In case of loss, please return to:

_____

_____

_____

_____

As a reward: $_____

CHASE THE GOOSE

RECLAIMING THE ADVENTURE OF LIVING A SPIRIT-LED LIFE

by Mark Batterson

Published by arrangement with WaterBrook Multnomah Publishing Group, a
division of Random House, Inc. © 2009 LifeWay Press®

ISBN: 978-1415-8676-62
Item: P005202109

Dewey Decimal Classification Number: 248.83
Subject Heading: CHRISTIAN LIFE \ GOD \ HOLY SPIRIT

Printed in the United States of America.

Leadership and Adult Publishing
LifeWay Church Resources
One LifeWay Plaza
Nashville, Tennessee 37234-0175

We believe the Bible has God for its author; salvation for its end; and truth,
without any mixture of error, for its matter and that all Scripture is totally true
and trustworthy. The 2000 statement of The Baptist Faith and Message is our
doctrinal guideline.

Cover designed by The Visual Republic.

TABLE of CONTENTS

SCALE 1 = 1 FT.
DRAWN BY.
TRACED BY
CHECKED BY

SKETCH SHEET

DATE

MEET *the* AUTHOR

MARK BATTERSON serves as lead pastor of National Community Church (*theaterchurch.com*) in Washington, D.C. NCC was recognized as one of the most innovative and most influential churches in America by *Outreach* magazine in 2008. One church with nine services in five locations, NCC is focused on reaching emerging generations. Approximately 70 percent of NCCers are single 20-somethings.

The vision of NCC is to meet in movie theaters at Metro™ stops throughout the D.C. area. NCC also owns and operates the largest coffeehouse on Capitol Hill. In 2008, Ebenezers was recognized as the best coffeehouse in the metro D.C. area by AOL CityGuide.

Mark has two master's degrees from Trinity Evangelical Divinity School in Chicago, Illinois. He is the author of a bestselling book, *In a Pit with a Lion on a Snowy Day*. His latest release is *Wild Goose Chase*. And he is a daily blogger at *markbatterson.com*.

Mark is married to Lora and they live on Capitol Hill with their three children: Parker, Summer, and Josiah.

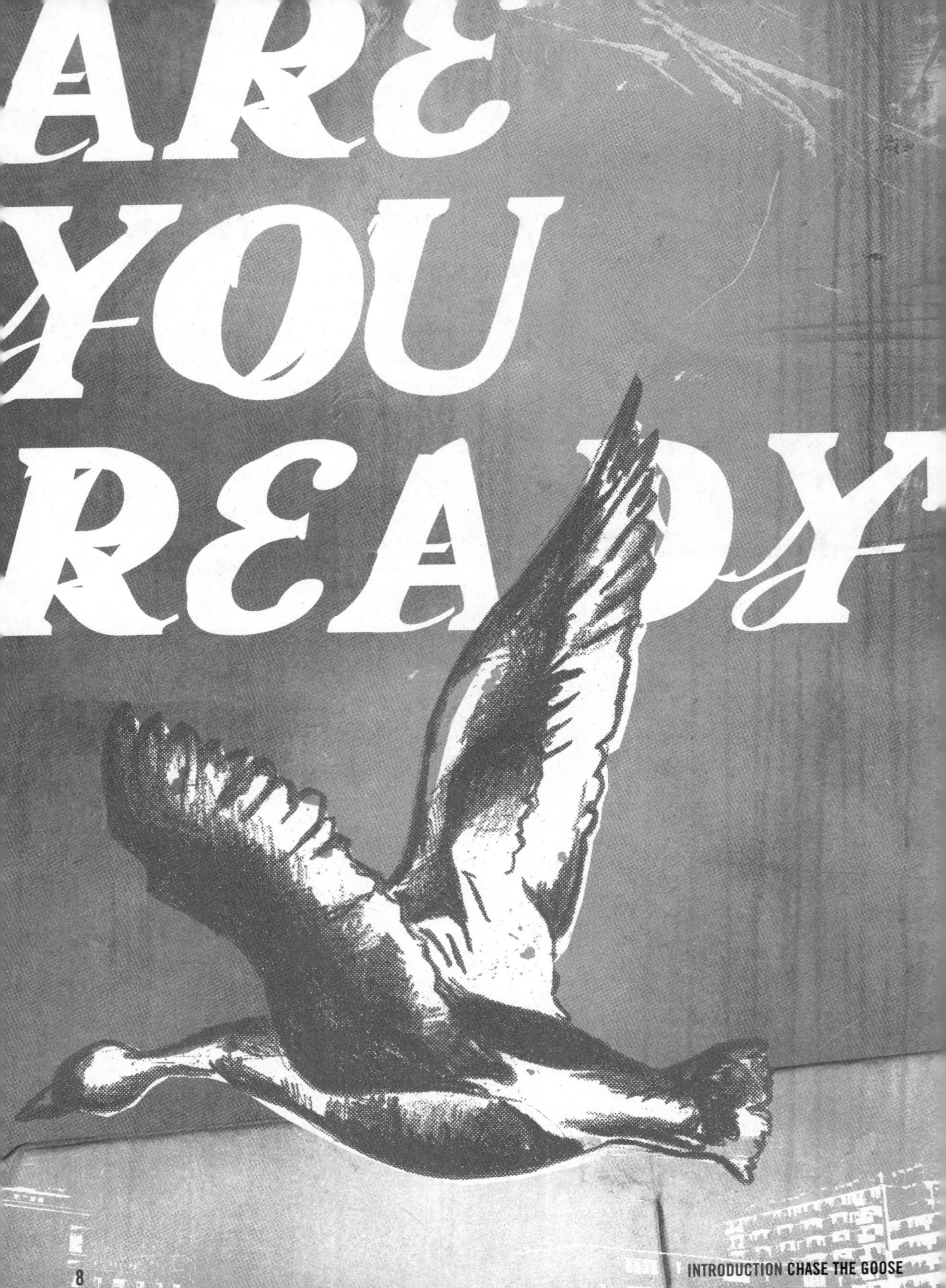
ARE
YOU
READY

ESCAPE

MOST OF US HAVE NO IDEA WHERE WE'RE GOING MOST OF THE TIME.

PERFECT.

CELTIC CHRISTIANS HAD A NAME FOR THE HOLY SPIRIT: *AN GEADH-GLAS,* **OR "THE WILD GOOSE." THE NAME HINTS AT MYSTERY. MUCH LIKE A WILD GOOSE, THE SPIRIT OF GOD CANNOT BE TRACKED OR TAMED.** An element of danger and an air of unpredictability surround Him. And while the name may sound a little sacrilegious, I can't think of a better description of what it's like to follow the Holy Spirit through life. The truth is: Most of us have no idea where we're going most of the time. I know that's unsettling, but circumstantial uncertainty goes by another name—*adventure.*

Have we clipped the wings of the Wild Goose and settled for something less than God intended? Are we missing out on what God created us to experience?

I realize the old adage "wild goose chase" typically refers to a purposeless endeavor without a defined destination. But chasing the Wild Goose is different. While the promptings of the Wild Goose may seem pointless at the time, God is constantly working His plan behind the scenes. If you chase the Wild Goose, you'll find yourself in places you could never have imagined along paths you never knew existed.

Have you ever gotten stressed out trying to determine the will of God for your life? We try to determine God's will like we try to solve puzzles, but often the will of God is neither linear nor logical. In Isaiah 55:8-9, God declares:

"FOR MY THOUGHTS ARE NOT YOUR THOUGHTS, AND YOUR WAYS ARE NOT MY WAYS . . . FOR AS HEAVEN IS HIGHER THAN EARTH, SO MY WAYS ARE HIGHER THAN YOUR WAYS, AND MY THOUGHTS THAN YOUR THOUGHTS."

I think it's only fair that we post a "Wild Goose Warning" at the beginning of this study: *Nothing is more unnerving or disorienting than passionately pursuing God.* In good conscience, I can't promise you safety or certainty, but I can promise that chasing the Wild Goose will be anything but boring. The sooner we come to terms with that spiritual reality, the more we will enjoy the journey.

CAGED CHRISTIANS

A few years ago, I visited the Galápagos Islands, where I experienced nature like I'd never experienced it before. I saw wild animals in their natural habitat—marine iguanas and 200-year-old Tortugas—and I went snorkeling with manta rays and swimming with sea lions. Two weeks later, I visited the National Zoo with my kids. We saw hundreds of interesting animals, but it just wasn't the same. The National Zoo is a great zoo, but it's a radically different experience to see a wild animal in a cage. It was too tame, too safe, and too civilized.

MANY PEOPLE LIVE AN INVERTED FORM OF CHRISTIANITY, TRYING TO GET GOD TO SERVE THEIR PURPOSES INSTEAD OF THEM TRYING TO SERVE HIS PURPOSES. IN WHAT WAYS DO YOU LIVE THAT WAY?

As we walked through the ape house, I wondered, *Have churches done to people what zoos do to animals? Have churches tried to tame Christians in the name of Christ?* I think so. We try to remove the risk, struggle, and danger from following Jesus, and we end up with caged Christians. Yes, it's a safe and comfortable environment, but I think deep down inside of us there's a longing for something more. That's what the Wild Goose chase is all about—chasing after the Wild Goose in order to live our lives the way God originally intended.

In this study, we will identify six cages that keep us from living the spiritual adventure God designed for us.

1. THE CAGE OF RESPONSIBILITY. Our God-ordained passions can get buried beneath day-to-day responsibilities. The Wild Goose chase begins when we start practicing responsible irresponsibility and come to terms with our greatest responsibility—pursuing the passions God has planted in our hearts. In this session, we go to work with a guy named Nehemiah, who walked away from some pretty important job responsibilities in order to embrace more important responsibilities.

WHAT IS YOUR GUT REACTION TO THE CELTIC DESCRIPTION OF THE WILD GOOSE AS UNTAMED AND UNPREDICTABLE?

2. THE CAGE OF ROUTINE. At some point in our journey, most of us trade adventure for routine. Some routines, like spiritual disciplines, can be good and actually help us become the people God intended. But if sacred practices become routine, they need to be disrupted and reworked. Otherwise, they become empty rituals, and we find ourselves trapped. In this session, we journey to the wilderness of Sinai with Moses, who was willing to throw down his staff, walk away from his sheep, and start shepherding God's people.

3. THE CAGE OF ASSUMPTIONS. As we age, many of us stop believing and start assuming. In this session, we join Abraham for a little stargazing to catch a glimpse of what is possible when you consider God in the equation of life.

4. THE CAGE OF GUILT. The enemy's tactics haven't changed since the garden of Eden. He tries to neutralize us spiritually by getting us to focus on what we've done wrong in the past. As long as we are trapped by the guilt of what we've done wrong, we're blinded to the dreams God has in mind for us. In this session, we follow Peter from the upper room to the courtyard of the high priest to the shore of Galilee and learn how Jesus can recondition our minds and hearts.

5. THE CAGE OF FAILURE. Sometimes our plans have to fail in order for God's plans to succeed. Divine detours and delays are often the paths God uses to get us where He wants us to go. This is the place where the Wild Goose chase will begin for many of us. In this session, we join Paul and other shipwreck survivors on the island of Malta to understand how our failure might turn into someone else's miracle.

6. THE CAGE OF FEAR. We need to quit living as if the purpose of life is to arrive safely at death. Instead, we need to start playing offense with our lives because the world needs more people with more daring plans. In this session, we scale the wall with Jonathan, look the opposition in the eye, and dare to do dangerous things.

OF THE SIX CAGES DESCRIBED, WHICH ONE DO YOU THINK MOST APPLIES TO YOUR LIFE? WHY?

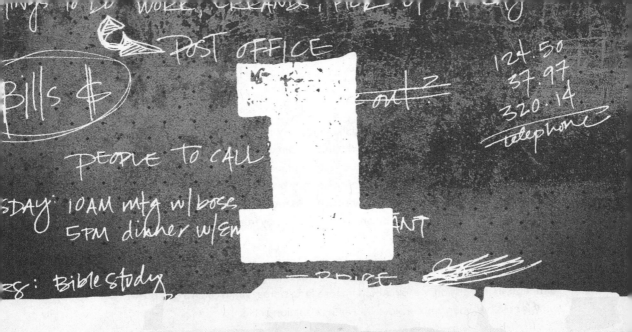

THE CAGE OF
RESPONSIBILITY

OVER THE COURSE OF OUR LIFETIMES, WE ASSUME A LOT OF RESPONSIBILITIES. If we aren't careful, the lesser responsibilities overtake the most important ones. If that happens, eventually we will realize we have formed a cage around ourselves with bars made out of stuff we "have to do." To break free from this cage, we must move from being irresponsibly responsible to responsibly irresponsible.

In August 2008, I went to Scotland with a few members of National Community Church to speak at a conference. While there, we stayed on the Royal Mile and found ourselves just a few blocks from Edinburgh Castle. As you enter the main gate of the castle, you see a plaque devoted to William Wallace. That plaque brought back memories of one of my all-time favorite movie scenes and quotes. William Wallace invested his life fighting for the freedom of his people. Just prior to being tortured to death, Wallace faced the choice of renouncing his beliefs or dying for them. His answer? "Every man dies, not every man really lives." And he faced death with the knowledge that "I have lived life to the fullest." That's how I want to live my life.

William Wallace was a Scottish knight and freedom-fighter known for leading a resistance during the Wars of Scottish Independence in the late 1200s and early 1300s. You can watch William Wallace give up personal responsibilities in order to fight and ultimately lose his life for Scottish Independence in the 1995 Oscar-winning movie, *Braveheart*.

According to *census.gov*, the life expectancy of an American born after 2005 is approximately 78 years.

PREMATURE DEATH

This may be a morbid way to begin this study, but it's always best to start with the end in mind. Ecclesiastes 3:1-2a states, "There is an occasion for everything, and a time for every activity under heaven: a time to give birth and a time to die." Ecclesiastes 7:2 elaborates the point saying, " . . . death is the destiny of every man; the living should take this to heart" (NIV). Given that death is an absolute certainty, I have to wonder: *What words would you want written on your tombstone? What life highlights would you like to see memorialized in your obituary?*

Complete one or more of the following statements:
- **I left the world a better place because . . .**

- **I changed someone's life by . . .**

- **God will say "well done good and faithful servant" because I . . .**

- **When I'm gone, people will remember that I . . .**

All of us were born, and all of us will die. We have a birth certificate and our family will one day be given our death certificate. But sadly, most people die long before the date on their death certificate. Premature death happens in lots of ways. For some people, pain, brokenness, or loss robs them of life. The enemy of their soul comes to steal, kill, and destroy, and their life is taken away. For others, disappointment and failure eat away the life inside them.

But for many of us, it happens in much more subtle ways. We find ourselves locked inside the cage of responsibility. Our day-to-day responsibilities numb us to the possibilities around us and the passions within us. And it happens slowly. Most of us don't even know how or when it started, but at some point, if we're honest, we stop living and start dying. It's almost like we are buried alive by our pain or disappointment or failure or debt . . . or responsibility.

Do you feel buried alive under anything right now? If so, what?

There's nothing wrong with responsibility. I have responsibilities as a husband, father, and pastor, and I need to embrace those responsibilities. We need to fulfill our responsibilities. We need to take out the trash, save for retirement, and pay our bills. But while we're doing those things, we can find ourselves buried alive by our day-to-day responsibilities and can totally miss out on the opportunities for spiritual adventure all around us. What I'm talking about is epitomized by one encounter in the Gospels.

In Matthew 8, Jesus invited a young man to follow Him, but the young man responded negatively (and responsibly):

"Lord . . . first let me go bury my father." And Jesus said, "Follow Me, and let the dead bury their own dead" (Matthew 8:21-22).

Now Bible scholars have a few different takes on what happened that day. It's possible the young man was putting off following Jesus until his father died. Maybe his father was sick and the young man was just waiting until that moment. Or maybe he didn't want to follow Jesus because he wanted to ensure he received his father's inheritance. Or perhaps he was afraid of abdicating his responsibilities in the family business while his father was still living.

Why do you think the man asked to bury his father? Can you sympathize with him?

Regardless, I feel a little sorry for him, don't you? I mean, what's so wrong with his request? It seems reasonable and responsible for this young man to look out for his family and bury his father. But when we're tempted to sympathize with someone other than Jesus, when something doesn't make sense, or when we sense a little dis-equilibrium, we need to take a closer look at the story. We need to drill down a little and try to figure out what's really happening and why we're feeling the way we're feeling.

Here's my take. I think this young man was doing what many of us do. He turned responsibility into an excuse. And Jesus saw through the smokescreen. The young man was allowing an arguably legitimate responsibility—burying his father—to get in the way of embracing his greatest responsibility and experiencing his greatest opportunity— following Christ.

To wrestle with other difficult statements in Scripture, check out *The Tough Sayings of Jesus* and *The Tough Sayings of Jesus II,* also from Threads (*threadsmedia.com*).

Burial of the dead is extremely important in Judaism. In fact, the process is so important that one is even excused from other religious duties to accomplish it. Consider this statement from the Talmud, a Jewish text second in importance only to the Hebrew Scriptures: "He who is confronted by a dead relative is freed from reciting the Shema, from the Eighteen Benedictions, and from all the commandments stated in the Torah."[1]

We do the same thing. We turn our responsibilities into excuses. We allow less important responsibilities to replace more important ones, and we find ourselves practicing irresponsible responsibility. One of the challenges of following Christ is to flip this tendency on its head and become responsibly irresponsible.

> Do you consider yourself to be more irresponsibly responsible or responsibly irresponsible? What's the difference between the two?

> Describe a time in your life when you used responsibility as an excuse to keep you from doing what God was calling you to do.

> List 10 responsibilities you currently have in your job, church, circle of friends, family, finances, etc. Which of those are you willing to give up to pursue something God might lead you to do?

So how do we become responsibly irresponsible? I think we can learn some lessons from the life of Nehemiah. Here's a little back-story. In 586 B.C., King Nebuchadnezzar invaded Judea and took many of the Jewish people back to Babylon as captives. In 538 B.C., Zerubbabel led the first remnant, about 43,000 Jews, back to Jerusalem. In 458 B.C., Ezra returned with a remnant of about 18,000, and Nehemiah showed up around 445 B.C.

The bottom line is this: Nehemiah found the wall of Jerusalem in total disrepair. This was significant because walls were the first and last lines of defense for ancient cities. Basically, the city of Jerusalem was defenseless. God conceived a passion in the spirit of Nehemiah, a cupbearer in Babylon, to return to Jerusalem and rebuild the wall.

Against all odds, he rebuilt the wall of the city in 52 days and went on to serve as governor of Jerusalem for more than a decade.

Nehemiah's life is a great model for us as we seek to break free from the cage of responsibility and practice responsible irresponsibility.

PAY ATTENTION TO PASSIONS

In order to break free from the cage of responsibility, we need to pay attention to the passions of our hearts. In Nehemiah 1:2, Nehemiah asked his brothers how things were going in Jerusalem. Although Nehemiah served in the king's palace, his heart remained in Jerusalem and the vision God gave him was tied to the passions of his heart. God has given each of us unique gifts, passions, and opportunities, and we should pay attention to those things because our calling is often found in them.

Chasing the Wild Goose starts with a single desire. Somehow this cupbearer got it in his mind and in his spirit that perhaps God might be calling him to do something about the problem in Jerusalem. But Nehemiah wasn't actually qualified to do anything about it. As far as we know, he had never even been to Jerusalem, and we don't know if he had the education or the experience that would qualify him to go and do anything close to the magnitude of a major building project.

In fact, his brother, Hanani, had a far better résumé for such a task. Why not him? Or why not the remnant back in Jerusalem? Why a cupbearer in Babylon? It doesn't make sense to me, but I know this—God conceives passions within us that sometimes seem crazy and that sometimes seem irresponsible. But it's the people who are willing to act on those God-breathed passions who truly make a difference.

> **Is there anything that you feel God may be calling you to do but you feel unqualified to do it? Why are you passionate about that thing?**

Can you identify your God-ordained passion? I think most people don't get what they want because they really don't know what they want. Because they don't, they never set any goals, never identify what their

Nehemiah lived at the same time as the spiritual leader Ezra. For more historical context, read the Book of Nehemiah alongside 1 and 2 Chronicles and Ezra. Ezra returned to Jerusalem 13 years before Nehemiah to rebuild the temple and restore the law. But these men understood it was just as important to rebuild the spiritual strength in the hearts of the people of God as it was to rebuild the physical wall around their city.

The cupbearer was an important official who served wine to the king. There was an ever-present danger of assassination by poisoning, so the cupbearer carried great responsibility. Such a person was intimately acquainted with the king he was entrusted to guard.

Check out *Repurposed: The Memoirs of Nehemiah* by Mike Hurt at *threadsmedia.com* for a Bible study centering on the principles from Nehemiah's life we can incorporate into the 21st-century church.

To dig a little deeper into the context of the Book of Nehemiah, read the articles called "The Purpose and Life-Situation of Nehemiah," "The King's 'Cupbearer,'" and "Nehemiah's Adversaries." They're found in the *Chase the Goose* leader kit, and your group leader will e-mail them to you this week.

passions are, and never define a dream. Passion is an emotional issue, both for you and for God. In fact, I would suggest that if you don't have a God-ordained passion, you are out of touch with the emotion and heart of God. So how do you identify those passions? How do you know they are from God? And how do you act on them?

As we continue to read Nehemiah 1, we discover that, upon hearing the news about Jerusalem, Nehemiah "sat down and wept" and "mourned for a number of days" (Nehemiah 1:4).

I once had a professor who asked some great questions. It's one of the few things I remember from graduate school, but I'll never forget when he said, "If you want to identify a passion, ask yourself these questions: What makes you cry or pound your fist on the table? What makes you sad? What makes you mad?"

I would throw one more into the mix: What makes you smile? God-ordained passions are found somewhere in the mixture of those emotions, and so you need to pay close attention to them.

What makes you cry?

What makes you mad?

What makes you smile?

Can you find examples in Scripture to demonstrate that God has the same reactions as you to the items you listed?

Can you identify the intersection of your greatest passion and the world's deepest need? If so, where is it?

Here's the thing: You never know how a God-ordained passion is going to develop in your spirit. It may be from a book you read, a mission trip, the newspaper, or a Google search. It could even be from a loss, like a death or a divorce. An experience like that can break you, but it can also conceive a passion within you. Regardless, you need to expose yourself to what's going on around the world—the good things and the bad things. You need to cry, you need to get mad, you need to find joy, and through it all, you need to allow God to get a hold of your heart. Often, that process means escaping from the context you live in—this cage of responsibility you've built for yourself.

Write down three issues you want to learn more about.

Sometimes we're afraid to ask questions because we realize knowing the answer will make us accountable to take action. Given that, write down one question that you need to know the answer to.

48 Days to the Work You Love by Dan Miller is a helpful guide in asking questions about passion and finding out where that passion fits into your career. Find out more at *48days.com*.

For Nehemiah, it all started with a conversation about the state of Jerusalem. But here's the thing—for a lot of us, such a conversation would have gone in one ear and out the other, and we would have simply said, "That's too bad." But for Nehemiah, it wasn't that simple. He was sensitive enough to allow God to conceive something within him. I don't know exactly how it happened, but let me just remind you that passions like this aren't about you discovering; they're really about God revealing.

The pressure isn't on you to figure it out all by yourself. If you're seeking to glorify God, if you want to live on mission, if you want Christ to be at the center of your life, if you are dwelling on the Word of God, if you are praying, if you are worshiping, if you are sensitive to the Spirit of God, He will reveal those things. He is going to conceive passion within your spirit.

The Hebrew word we translate as "delight" is *anag*, and its meaning carries with it the idea of being soft and pliable as we take delight in God.

There are eight references made to prayer in the Book of Nehemiah. Can you find them?

I love Psalm 37:4 because it gets to the heart of what I'm saying: "Take delight in the LORD, and He will give you your heart's desires." The word *give* actually means "to conceive." I suppose if you wanted a technological analogy, it might mean to download. When you delight yourself in the Lord, He begins to download new desires within you. He places passions in you that might seem unexplainable at first. And though you don't really have a handle on it, you feel like God is doing something deep inside you.

But here's a word of caution: I think figuring out what you want—even what God wants for you—can turn into a very selfish endeavor. So you'd better make sure what you want is what God wants. How do you do that? I wish I had a formula; I don't. But again, I'm confident that if your life is saturated in the Word of God, and if you're sensitive to the Spirit of God, He's going to lead you into those things He wants you to be passionate about. That's the "delighting yourself in God" part. If you delight yourself in God, He's going to give you the desires of your heart. As you grow in a relationship with God, those God-ordained passions are going to grow deep inside of you.

PRAY AND PREPARE

So Nehemiah "mourned for a number of days, fasting and praying before the God of heaven" (Nehemiah 1:4). He confessed his sins, his family's sins, and the sins of Israel. He recalled history and prayerfully considered the ways God had worked in Israel's past (Nehemiah 1:5-10). Nehemiah's vision was birthed and bathed in prayer.

Nehemiah was willing to wait on God's timing. He received the news of the wall in the Hebrew month of Kislev, which was most likely November or December. He did not leave for Jerusalem until the Hebrew month of Nisan, or April. He waited patiently and prayerfully for four to five months until the time was right. Sometimes, the hardest part of passion is the waiting. We get mad or sad or glad and we want to immediately go out and start doing something about it. But sometimes we have to wait.

Three days after Nehemiah arrived in Jerusalem, he went out to survey the wall. At that point, he hadn't told "anyone what my God had laid on my heart to do for Jerusalem" (Nehemiah 2:12). Nehemiah did not communicate his vision or go public until he gathered the facts, received direction from God, and formulated a plan. In Nehemiah 2:16, he said:

"The officials did not know where I had gone or what I was doing, for I had not yet told the Jews, priests, nobles, officials, or the rest of those who would be doing the work."

Nehemiah moved slowly and wisely through the hard work of hearing from God and personally preparing for the vision before going public.

Personal preparation often begins years before we start actively pursuing or living in our God-ordained passion and calling. Nehemiah obviously worked well for many years as the cupbearer. As cupbearer, he was trusted by the king. And when it was time to go public, his relationship with the king paid huge dividends.

To prepare ourselves during the waiting period, we should focus on developing godly character and being faithful in the little things. Nehemiah had a passion to rebuild the walls of Jerusalem. But he wasn't an architect or a mason. He wasn't a great leader of people. He was a cupbearer, the trusted official who tasted food and drink for the king to make sure it wasn't poisoned. But in the meantime, he decided to continue to be the best cupbearer he could be.

Likewise, you may find yourself far from the passion God has given you, but you can choose to be the best cupbearer you can be. After all, if you are faithful in Babylon, God will bless you in Jerusalem.

> **What is the "Babylon" you need to be faithful in right now? What does that look like, practically?**

This idea of waiting on God runs throughout Scripture. Noah worked on the Ark for 100 years. Abraham lived for 25 years between the calling of God and the birth of Isaac. David worked several odd jobs for many years between being anointed king of Israel and assuming the throne. The lame man at the pool of Bethesda waited 38 years to be healed. Can you think of other examples?

Here's one example. Some time ago, I was in Ethiopia speaking at Beza International Church. As Pastor Zeb Mengistu prepared the congregation for the offering, he jokingly said that if someone wanted to write a seven-digit check, they could make it out to "Beza International Church." He was just joking with his congregation, but when he said it, something quickened in my spirit. I thought, *The day will come when NCC and I will write a seven-digit check to this church.* I can't totally explain it, but something was conceived in my spirit. I don't know when, I don't know how, but the day will come when National Community Church will invest a million dollars.

Visit Beza International Church online at *beza.publishpath.com*.

How does that start? Well, it starts with us giving $25,000 toward the AIDS outreach to the Entoto Outreach Project. It starts with us sending mission teams to serve the church and the community and make a difference. It starts with us being obedient in the little things. If we are obedient in the little things, then those big desires God conceives in our hearts will become reality. I believe that.

> **What is one small thing you can do this week to start being a solution?**

> **Choose one of the following prayers and pray it this week:**
> - **God stretch me.**
> - **God use me.**
> - **God break my heart.**

> **What little things do you need to be doing now to prepare yourself for the bigger things God wants you to do down the road?**

SPRING INTO ACTION

To pursue his vision, Nehemiah was required to leave his position in the court of King Artaxerxes and to relocate to Jerusalem. To pursue his greater responsibility, he had to become responsibly irresponsible by leaving his job and the security of what he knew. He had to say no to one thing in order to say yes to something else.

The king not only gave Nehemiah permission to leave his post to rebuild the wall in Jerusalem, he also granted Nehemiah safe travel and sent army officers and cavalry for protection. In addition, he donated timber from the royal forest for construction (Nehemiah 2:7-9).

When God puts a passion in your heart, you need to take responsibility for it even if it means becoming irresponsible somewhere else. I think that's the gap. That's where so often the kingdom doesn't really advance because we choose responsibility over spiritual adventure, and we never act on the passion God has put in our hearts. Whether the passion is to address human trafficking in a third-world country, provide inner-city education, or make movies with redemptive messages, you need to take responsibility for it. You need to own it. You need to see the problem and then become a part of the solution.

It was irresponsible for Nehemiah to give up his position. He had a great job. He was the cupbearer to the king. He was a trusted and influential member of the royal administration, and it probably looked like he was throwing away a great position. Some might even say he was throwing away what looked like a God-ordained position. But Nehemiah knew something so many of us have to learn the hard way—if you succeed at the wrong thing, you fail. All of us know successful failures don't we? They're people who are really successful and really unhappy. Successful failures are people who succeed at things that don't really matter and lack fulfillment at the end of the day. My heart breaks for those people.

Stephen Covey said you can climb the ladder of success and then realize it's leaning against the wrong wall.[3] I think Nehemiah could've climbed all the way up the ladder of success, and at the top, if it wasn't leaning on the wall of Jerusalem, felt like a total failure because he hadn't pursued what God had called him to do.

> **What wall is your success ladder currently leaning against? What wall should it be leaning against?**

The Wild Goose will show up in wild places at wild times, and He will take you places you never imagined going by paths you never knew existed—if you are open to Him conceiving those God-ordained passions in your heart. But once that passion is conceived in your heart, you need to do something about it.

According to cognitive neuroscientists, we process information in a couple of different ways. Some things we process from the bottom-up, from primal parts of the human brain. This is the process by which the amygdala has an emotional response to situations. The second type of neurological processing is top-down. The prefrontal cortex and the more developed parts of the human brain begin to get involved in the process. Both bottom-up and top-down processes are amazing. Top-down processing is a wonderful thing, but it's possible to over-think. Anyone with a background in athletics knows what I'm talking about. It's choking when you're trying to kick a game-winning field goal or sink the final free throw. If you over-think, you're in trouble because it's probably not going to work out.

When you're given a God-ordained passion, you need to talk about it, you need to think about it, and you need to pray about it. Jesus said you need to count the cost, and that's top-down processing. But we need to be very careful because a lot of us are trying to over-talk, over-think, and (dare I say) over-pray, when God wants us to act.

Becoming responsibly irresponsible means we have to cheat somewhere, and we need to be careful we don't cheat or become irresponsible with the wrong things. Check out *Choosing to Cheat* by Andy Stanley to read more about how and who to cheat responsibly.

Dr. Stephen Covey has been recognized as one of *Time* magazine's 25 most influential Americans. His core message is that every person can truly control their destiny with profound, yet straightforward, guidance. Find out more at *stephencovey.com*.

Andy Stanley writes about the leadership principles from the account of Nehemiah in *Visioneering*. Consider picking up a copy to help you develop a vision for what God has in store for you.

At your small group meeting time this week, watch the short film "Polaroids." Can you see yourself in the situation presented?

National Community Church is recognized as one of the most innovative churches in the country. Its vision is to meet in movie theaters at Metro™ stops throughout the metro D.C. area. Check it out at *theaterchurch.com*.

Let me be blunt: Sometimes we need to stop praying and start doing.

What are some general things that we don't need to pray about?

What are some things you personally need to stop praying about and start doing?

In the last verse of Mark's Gospel, Mark 16:20, we read:

"And they went out and preached everywhere, the Lord working with them and confirming the word by the accompanying signs."

I think most of us want signs to precede any action we take: *God give me a sign, then I'll step out in faith.* But generally that's not how God works. The result is that we spend our lives waiting for God while God is waiting for us. And we wonder why God isn't making the move and God is wondering why we aren't making the move.

I remember when our church consisted of about 25 people and we were meeting in a Washington, D.C., public school. I was leading worship. It was bad. We didn't have a drummer and I have no rhythm. We prayed for a drummer. We prayed for a drummer *forever.* One morning, I felt like God spoke to me and told me to go buy a drum set. I said, "We don't have a drummer." But I went out and bought a $400 drum set. I didn't have a lot of faith, but on Sunday, three days after that step of faith, a guy from the United States Marine Drum and Bugle Corps showed up and became our first drummer. Is that coincidence? I don't think so.

Or how about this—several years ago, Ebenezers Coffeehouse was just a crazy idea. Today, it is the largest coffeehouse in D.C. and a huge outreach and ministry of our church. It all began at a school auction for my kids. I found a three-inch thick binder from the Capitol Hill Restoration Society with all the Capitol Hill zoning regulations. Needless to say, no one else bid on it. But I had been researching regulations and zoning and trying to figure out if we could build a coffeehouse at 201 F Street. By faith, for $65 bucks, I bought that zoning manual. And I still have it because it was a step of faith and God honored it.

When you step out, God will begin to work. So enough talking already—*do something*. Buy a book, make an appointment, enroll in a class, or write a check. I don't know what it may be for you, but you need to do something, and you need to do it now.

The wall of Jerusalem didn't rebuild itself. Nehemiah had to step out and get busy. And as soon as he started stepping forward, he faced opposition. When you begin living a life of responsible irresponsibility, you will receive criticism, face opposition, and encounter obstacles.

> **Skim Nehemiah 4–6. What were some of the obstacles and criticism that were thrown into Nehemiah's path?**

> **How did he respond and what lessons can you learn from him?**

When the critics Tobiah, Sanballat, and Geshem requested a meeting with Nehemiah, he responded with one of my favorite quotes in Scripture: "I am doing a great work and cannot come down. Why should the work cease while I leave it and go down to you?" (Nehemiah 6:3).

> **How can you tell the difference between godly criticism and negative criticism?**

IMAGINE...

Nehemiah and his team completed the wall in 52 days, culminating in several celebrations—the reading of the law, the festival of booths, and a public confession of sin. Nehemiah's bold decision to act responsibly irresponsible resulted in revival.

If you are ever in Washington, D.C., swing by Ebenezers Coffeehouse, located one block from Union Station. Or check it out online at *ebenezerscoffeehouse.com*.

The leader of the critics was a guy named Sanballat. If the name itself isn't bad enough, its meaning is even worse. His name means "sin gives life."

Imagine a church full of people pursuing God's ordained passions. A church like that would change a city. Imagine a campus ministry full of people pursuing God-ordained passions. A ministry like that would change a university. If all of us came out of the cage of responsibility and actually took responsibility for the things that make us mad or sad or glad, we would turn our neighborhoods and nations upside down. We would actually *be* the kingdom of God.

In his inaugural address, President Kennedy challenged the American people, "Ask not what your country can do for you—ask what you can do for your country." The Peace Corp program emerged from that challenge. In the past year, the number of volunteers in their 50s and older has risen by 50 percent. One of these Peace Corps baby boomers is 64-year-old Loyci Stockey, who said, "I never forgot his message, and I tucked it away in the back of my head to act on someday. Today is my someday."[4] That's a powerful statement.

Today is your someday, but you need to act. That first act may seem small and insignificant, but remember Rome wasn't built in a day and it took 52 days to rebuild the wall of Jerusalem. It's not going to happen overnight, but you've got to start somewhere. You need to count the cost, step out in faith, and do something small. I'm not saying you should ignore all the responsibilities you have. But at some point, you've got to consider whether or not you're being responsible about the right things.

So what is the Wild Goose saying? What is God conceiving in your spirit? And are you willing to step out? The bottom line is that your greatest responsibility is pursuing God-ordained passions. If you over-think it, it'll never happen.

What is it that makes you mad or sad or glad? If you're struggling to answer that question, then follow Nehemiah's lead and spend a few days praying and seeking God, examining the walls, and getting a sense of what God is calling you to. It might not happen overnight. Don't get frustrated if you can't figure it out quickly. I just turned 39, and I'm still figuring out everything God has put inside me. Nevertheless, I believe that as I continue to grow in my relationship with God, He is going to conceive some things in my spirit that I can't even imagine right now. Don't let what you can't do keep you from doing what you can. Come out of that cage of responsibility and chase the Goose.

NOW WHAT?

PRAYER

Lord help us. Help us, I pray, to be a people of passion, a people who act on those passions that You have conceived in our lives. You invite us into the adventure of following You, and I pray that we would have the courage to accept that invitation. God, I pray for those who have become numb to the possibilities and the passions. Would You turn over the soil of our hearts so that we would begin to live the lives that You called us to? Begin a good work in us. Thank You that You are the One who carries it on to completion. Amen.

SCRIPTURE MEMORY

"Humble yourselves therefore under the mighty hand of God, so that He may exalt you in due time, casting all your care upon Him, because He cares about you" (1 Peter 5:6-7).

CHASING THE GOOSE

- Read *Holy Discontent* by Bill Hybels.
- Make a list of your daily, weekly, and monthly responsibilities. Evaluate each of them as to whether they are furthering or hindering your pursuit of the Wild Goose.
- Make an action plan taking into account the evaluation above, leaving room for the Wild Goose.

notes

2

SESSION TWO CHASE THE GOOSE

THE CAGE OF
ROUTINE

WHEN THE SACRED BECOMES ROUTINE, WE MISS THE ADVENTURE OF THE WILD GOOSE. It's good to have spiritual routines; we usually call them spiritual disciplines. But when our routines become routine, boredom ensues. Chasing the Wild Goose is never boring. In order to break free from the cage of routine, we need to shake up what happens in our lives, day in and day out.

At the end of our trip to the Galápagos Islands, we flew back to Ecuador and made a five-hour bus trip through the Andes Mountains from Guia to Cuenca, Ecuador. As we drove through the mountains, we couldn't see the peaks because of the cloud cover. The clouds formed a ceiling we couldn't see through. At about 12,000 feet, we finally drove through the clouds and our cloud ceiling turned into a celestial carpet. It was one of the most majestic sites I've ever seen. It was literally the closest I've ever come to feeling like I was on top of the world.

The Andes form the world's longest exposed mountain range. They lie on the western coast of South America where the range stretches 4,400 miles and has an average height of 13,000 feet.

THIN PLACES

When I got off the bus, I was so caught up in the majesty of God's creation that I started clapping because I didn't know what else to do. I guess I was so overwhelmed by the amazing site around me that I felt like the Creator deserved a round of applause.

Have you ever experienced a moment like that? Have you ever stood in the midst of pure wonder? It defies words. The Celtic Christians had a name for such places. They called them "thin places." They're places where heaven and earth seem to touch, where God seems to hold back the space-time curtain and reveal just a little bit more of His glory. They're places where and moments when the Wild Goose invades the reality of your life and you are changed forever.

> Have you ever experienced a "thin place"? If so, when and where?

> What was your dominant emotion?

> Why do you think God encountered you in that way and in that place?

The Midianites were descendants of Abraham through his wife Keturah. These are the same people who earlier bought Joseph from his brothers and sold him into slavery. They were a nomadic people living in the desert. It was unusual for Jethro, the man who became Moses' father-in-law, to extend hospitality to Moses, a Jew, since the Midianites were hostile to Israel.

BURNING BUSHES

Exodus 3 was a thin place in Moses' walk with God. A fugitive who, in his anger, killed an Egyptian task-master, Moses fled Egypt to a land called Midian where he spent 40 years on the backside of a desert tending sheep. I wonder if Moses felt forsaken or forgotten by God. Forty years is a long time to be on the backside of the desert, in the middle of nowhere, tending sheep.

That's where we pick up this story in Exodus 3:1:

"One day Moses was tending the flock of his father-in-law, Jethro, the priest of Midian, and he went deep into the wilderness near Sinai, the mountain of God. Suddenly, the angel of the LORD appeared to him as a

blazing fire in a bush. Moses was amazed because the bush was engulfed in flames, but it didn't burn up. 'Amazing!' Moses said to himself. 'Why isn't that bush burning up? I must go over to see this.' When the LORD saw that he had caught Moses' attention, God called to him from the bush, 'Moses! Moses!' 'Here I am!' Moses replied. 'Do not come any closer,' God told him. 'Take off your sandals, for you are standing on holy ground'" (Exodus 3:1-5, NLT).

Moses had been tending sheep for 40 years. That's 480 months, 2,080 weeks, or 14,560 days. He practiced the same daily routine for 40 years, day in and day out, and I think Moses probably felt like God had put him out to pasture. Was Moses a little bit disappointed with his life? Did he feel like an underachiever? Every day, he stared at the backsides of sheep—not very exciting. After that long, Moses must have been caught in the cage of routine.

List some of the routines in your life.

Are you troubled or disappointed by any of these routines? If so, why? Where do you feel like an underachiever?

While working as a shepherd for his father-in-law, Moses gained first-hand experience in and geographical knowledge of the area surrounding the Gulf of Aqaba, through which he would later lead the people of Israel.

But I love the first two words of this chapter. To me, they're words of incredible hope:

One day.

Those words epitomize what a relationship with Christ is all about. When you are in relationship with Jesus, all bets are off. You never know what you're going to do, where you're going to go, or who you're going to meet. You never know when or where or how God is going to invade the reality of your life and turn it inside out and upside down in a single moment. He can show up any place, any time, and turn your life into a Wild Goose chase. That fills me with holy anticipation. It changes the way I live my life because I can't wait to see what God is going to do next.

I don't want to paint a prettier picture of my own life than it really is, because I live in the daily routine, too. I can get caught in that cage, and sometimes life seems pretty monotonous. My days don't start in a glamorous way. I crawl out of bed, walk our dog Mickey, and pick up his poop. That's how my day starts. Every single one. But I do live with a deep-seeded, holy anticipation of what God is going to do because I never know how or when He will invade the ordinary reality of my life.

Describe a time when God invaded the reality of your life. When was it? Where were you? What happened?

In your experience, how does God typically work in your life—in "one day" moments, or over the course of a long, slow, steady process? Can you find biblical reasons to support your experience?

I think we read stories about people in the Bible with hindsight bias. In other words, we know the stories so well; we know how they start and how they end. And we can read them in a matter of minutes. Because the stories are so familiar, it's easy for us to assume the stories were just as familiar to the characters in them. I think it's important for us to realize that the people in these biblical adventures were just like you and me. They were living their lives as they always did, and God invaded those lives in ways they never expected. They had no clue the stories were going to happen the way they did.

For instance, you can't tell me that a farmer named Noah had any idea that around his 500th birthday he would build this really big boat. No clue!

I don't think a shepherd named David knew he would become king.

I don't think an orphan named Esther knew she would become a queen.

I don't think Elisha had any idea he'd become a prophet.

And I think Moses thought that he would tend sheep until the day he died. I think he literally felt unqualified and disqualified. He had no idea

(R)

Christian leaders have begun to refer to unique opportunities for the gospel in the day-to-day lives of Christ-followers as "divine appointments." To learn more about how to recognize those appointments, take a look at *Becoming a Contagious Christian* by Bill Hybels.

- Read Noah's story in Genesis 6:9–9:29.
- Read David's story in 1 Samuel 16:1-13.
- Read Esther's story in Esther 2:1-20.
- Read Elisha's story in 1 Kings 19:15-21.

he would go back to Egypt and confront Pharaoh. He had no idea he would reveal the glory of Israel's God through 10 miracles. And he had no idea he would be the one who, after 400 years of captivity, would lead the people of Israel out of Egypt and toward the promised land.

But *one day*.

One day, God showed up.

What is God asking you to do that you feel totally unqualified or disqualified to do? What makes you unqualified or disqualified?

At your small group meeting time this week, watch the short film "Lab Rats." It's an interesting look at what might happen if you can start to break out of the routine.

By the way, Jewish scholars used to debate why God revealed Himself in a burning bush on the backside of the desert. It seems like there would be better places or ways to reveal yourself if you're God. Lightning and thunderbolts are more impressive to me. Revealing yourself at the pyramids or Pharaoh's palace seem like more logical choices. Why a burning bush in the middle of nowhere? Jewish scholars came to this consensus—revelation at that time and that place was God's way of showing that no place is devoid of His presence. Not even a bush on the backside of the desert. He can show up any place, any time, and we need to live with that reality.

What places in your life seem devoid of the presence of God?

Not so long ago, I was a freshman at the University of Chicago. If you would have told me then that I would be living in Washington, D.C., and serving as a pastor of a church, I would have thought you were crazy. That idea wasn't in my conscience. It wasn't in my subconscious. I had no idea. Many of you reading this study are in college or are 20-somethings, and I daresay many of you have no idea where you are going to be in 10 years. That can be incredibly scary, can't it? But fear also goes by another name—adventure. Adventure is where the sovereignty of God comes into play, and you simply have to trust that the Wild Goose is going to get you where He wants you to go. Getting you to where He wants you to go is the business of the Wild Goose, and He's really good at it.

> **Have you ever experienced "adventure" in your life because you were chasing after God's will? If so, what happened?**

One day. I hope you'll live with that reality, with the hope that God can invade your life just like He invaded Moses'. The invasion of God can change everything in a moment.

> **List three areas of life in which you need to experience an invasion of God.**

Listen to "Live" by Nichole Nordeman on the *Chase the Goose* playlist. Your leader will send you the whole playlist via e-mail, or you can find it at *threadsmedia.com/chase-the-goose*. Use these songs as the background music for your study.

OUR RESPONSE

How would we respond in that situation? Can any of us predict how we would respond if God appeared to us in a burning bush? I don't know that I would have a very profound reaction. Notice what Moses did. He was caught a little off guard, but then he offered a simple, instinctual response: "Here I am."

God knew exactly where you were, Moses, but thanks for giving directions. However, I think that response is more than just an effort to identify his location. It's as though Moses was saying, after 40 years, "I am *here*. And while we're on that subject, what am I doing here? And what are you doing? I feel so forsaken and forgotten!"

Finally, God showed up and Moses said, "Here I am." This is where his Wild Goose chase began. But it wasn't immediate. God gave him instructions to release His people from slavery, and Moses put up some resistance. Then he second-guessed himself. Then he second-guessed God. But it all began with a simple, "Here I am."

If God called your name, how would you respond?

The Wild Goose chase is not just about some self-absorbed attempt at adventure; it is so much more than that. Two thousand years ago, Jesus extended an invitation, "Come follow me." That invitation is still on the table, and the Wild Goose chase begins the moment we put our faith in Christ and decide to follow Him. But many of us make the mistake of believing that Jesus *just* came to save us from our sin. Make no mistake—He does that. The moment we put our faith in Christ, when we confess our sins, "He is faithful and just and will forgive us our sins and purify us from all unrighteousness" (1 John 1:9, NIV). He takes care of the sin problem; He takes care of the past. But some of us live as if that's all He does and that's all He offers.

Life with Christ is so much more than that.

God takes care of the past to invite us into the future. He takes care of the past so we can realize the potential He has given to us and truly live the spiritual adventure the Wild Goose has planned and is calling us to join.

SAVE US FROM BOREDOM

Can I make a suggestion? God came to save us from boredom. Soren Kierkegaard said, "Boredom is the root of all evil."[5] I despise boredom. There won't be an ounce of boredom in heaven. There shouldn't be an ounce of boredom in our lives.

I want a shirt that says "boring is boring" or "nothing is more boring than boredom." Perhaps we should spell it "bore-dumb." Here's what I know for sure—the disciples never got bored. Jesus was predictably unpredictable. He was counterintuitive and countercultural, and so the disciples learned to expect the unexpected.

Look at this story of Moses at face value. Moses had to be bored out of his mind. Maybe occasionally his flock would get attacked by a wild animal, there would be a little rush of adrenaline, and it would be an exciting day for him. But the next day, it was back to staring at the backsides of sheep. I'm guessing that most days he was bored silly.

Soren Kierkegaard was a 19th-century Danish theologian and philosopher. Some of his more famous writings include *Works of Love, Christian Discourses,* and *Training in Christianity.*

List some areas of your life that have become boring.

God created us with adrenal glands. He's the One who designed us so that when we experience something exciting or adventurous, we experience a rush of adrenaline. Call me crazy, but I think adrenaline is a stewardship issue. I think we need to be good stewards of adrenaline just like we need to be good stewards of glucose or testosterone or dopamine or any other thing that God has put in us. *Everything* is a stewardship issue.

I define sin as meeting a legitimate need in an illegitimate way. I think a lot of us are bored silly with our relationship with God, so we try to get that rush of adrenaline in the wrong way. Moses got a rush of adrenaline when he killed that Egyptian taskmaster, but it was sinful.

You can find the story of how Moses killed the Egyptian in Exodus 2:11-15.

List some legitimate needs that people often meet in illegitimate ways.

What are some legitimate needs in your life that you are currently meeting in illegitimate ways?

Do you consider those to be sinful? Why or why not?

When God begins to redeem us and we say, "Here I am, and I'm going to chase the Wild Goose," something happens. Do you think Moses experienced a rush of adrenaline when he walked back in to confront Pharaoh? What about when he took that staff for the first time, threw it down, and it turned into a snake? It must have been a God-ordained rush of adrenaline. What about standing in front of the Red Sea with the Egyptian army breathing down his neck? What a rush that must have been! But the key is that it was a *holy* rush of adrenaline.

> **Describe the last time you experienced a rush of adrenaline from chasing the Wild Goose. If you've never experienced one, do you want to? What might be keeping you from experiencing a holy adrenaline rush?**

Adrenaline is a hormone released into the blood in order to rapidly prepare the body for action in emergency situations. The hormone boosts the supply of oxygen and glucose to the brain and muscles.

I wonder if we've missed that part of the story. The human side. The emotional side. It's so easy for us to read the stories of the Bible and miss what they're really about. Sure, God had a dynamic plan for Moses' life. He wanted to use him to deliver the Israelites. But God also wanted to do something *in* Moses. When Moses had nothing on his agenda except sheep, God came to the rescue and saved him from his boredom. God invaded the reality of his life. I want to experience life like that.

GETTING OUR ATTENTION

As we continue to read the passage, we notice a significant phrase in verse 4. Moses was tending sheep and saw the bush:

"When the LORD saw that he had caught Moses' attention, God called to him from the bush, 'Moses! Moses!'"

The simple fact that God had to capture Moses' attention tells me that God had lost Moses' attention. Or at least that Moses had stopped paying attention to God. I think that's what routine does.

If you want to dig a little deeper into Moses' setting when he encountered the burning bush, read the article "Midian: The Land and Its People." Your group leader can e-mail it to you this week.

Routine is a good thing. We need routine. Without routine, life is absolutely chaotic. Most of us have a morning routine that involves a shower and toothpaste and deodorant. On behalf of your friends and family, continue with that routine. It's a good thing.

But here's the catch 22: once a routine becomes a routine, you need to disrupt the routine.

Let me put it in physiological terms. If you work out your muscles in the same way every time you go to the gym, eventually your muscles will adapt to the routine and you will stop getting stronger. In order to continue developing at that point, you have to confuse your muscles

To learn more about the spiritual disciplines, pick up a copy of *The Life You've Always Wanted* by John Ortberg. You'll find the disciplines aren't super-spiritual, but ways for everyday people to connect with God.

We are instructed to sing a new song to the Lord six times in the Psalms—Psalm 33:3, 40:3, 96:1, 98:1, 144:9, and Psalm 149:1.

by disrupting the routine in order for your body to respond. The same thing is true of spiritual routines or "spiritual disciplines"—things like prayer, fasting, Bible study, and fellowship. When you begin practicing these disciplines, it's easy to forget why you're doing them in the first place. At some point you stop worshiping God in spirit and in truth and just go through the motions; it's almost like you are simply lip-synching the words. Instead of really worshiping from a place deep in your soul where you really think about what you're singing, you just mindlessly and heartlessly mouth empty words.

I read a study finding that after you sing a song 30 times, you no longer think about the lyrics. That has huge ramifications when it comes to worship. Maybe that's why the psalmists encouraged the people of God six times throughout the Book of Psalms to sing to the Lord a *new* song. But the principle goes beyond worship; it happens in all areas of spiritual growth. You start living out of left-brain memory instead of right-brain imagination. You stop creating a future and start repeating the past, and your life becomes an empty ritual that doesn't mean anything.

Is it possible God might be telling us something like, "Hey, I'm over here!"? God uses different circumstances in our lives to get our attention. Sometimes He gets our attention through tragedy—the death of a loved one, divorce papers, a diagnosis, or something else that shakes us to the core. Sometimes that's what it takes for us to ask what's going on, what's my life about, and whether there's a God at all.

It doesn't always have to come to that. There are things we can do to disrupt the routine of our lives. We know we should read our Bibles, pray, and practice a number of other spiritual disciplines. But maybe there are some ways to maintain the discipline while changing up the routine.

What parts of your spiritual life are being lived out of memory instead of imagination?

What are some ways you can change up your spiritual routine?

What is the connection between "one day" transformation and the transformation that comes over the long haul implementation of spiritual disciplines in your life?

READ A NEW TRANSLATION

In order to change up the routine, you might start simply: Try a new translation of the Bible. Different words cause different synapses to fire in your brain. It's a very simple, neurological principle. The problem is that many of us have read the same version of the Bible so many times that we tune out; we don't think about it because we know exactly how it's going to end. This is a really small change, but I've found that rejuvenating my devotional life is sometimes as quick and easy as changing the translation.

START A FAST

Fasting is giving up something for the purpose of seeking God. It's about seeking God with intensity and dependency. Consider doing a 40-day fast. Forty isn't a magic number, but it does seem to have some biblical significance. Jesus fasted for 40 days. The children of Israel wandered for 40 years. Maybe "40" is something you work up to. In the beginning, though, you might try to fast from something for 3 days. Or 7 days. Or 21 days. Regardless, I think fasting is one of those overlooked, under-practiced spiritual disciplines we read about but no one really does.

We've experimented with fasting as a congregation at National Community Church. Personally, I try to do a couple of fasts every year. Sometimes it's a 10-day fast beginning on New Year's Day. Sometimes I fast over Lent. If I am moving into a new season or I want God to prepare me for what He wants to do next in my life, I will fast. I have also found that fasting is a great way to break or build a habit. You can fast *food* or fast *fast food*. Or you can fast other things, like television or e-mail or a hobby. It's a great way to mix up the routine.

Write down an activity you can eliminate from your life this week that will help you focus more on chasing the Wild Goose.

When choosing a Bible translation, you have to find the balance between accuracy and readability. Accuracy is the closeness of the translation to the original text. Readability is the relevance of the language of the translation today. In general, the more accurate the translation, the less readable it is; and the more readable the translation, the less accurate. The New International Version is generally believed to be the best balance of accuracy and readability. The Holman Christian Standard Bible is also a great blend of accuracy and readability.

A Hunger for God is John Piper's extensive explanation of the biblical mandate, process, and benefits of fasting.

Choosing the right venue for journaling is important. If a nice, leather-bound book would make you feel pressure to write consistently "profound" thoughts, then just go with a plain spiral-bound notebook. On the other hand, if it is important to you to make the journaling experience significant and special, consider investing in a nice notebook and writing instrument.

KEEP A JOURNAL

Start recording your thoughts in some sort of journal. It could be a gratitude journal, a prayer journal, or a dream journal. It could be a journal of the daily record of what God is doing in your life or notes about what you are learning as you read through the Bible. You may know people who have been Christians for 25 years, but they don't have 25 years of experience. They have one year of experience repeated 25 times because they aren't learning the lessons that God is trying to teach them. Why? Because they never really stop to think about them.

I've always journaled because I've found that it is one key to processing what God is trying to do in my life, and it keeps life from becoming routine. When I begin my day jotting down three things that I'm grateful for in my gratitude journal, it makes the day anything but routine. Why? Because I am noticing what God is doing and I am celebrating His blessing; and that makes all the difference in the world. Remember, the shortest pencil is longer than the longest memory.

GO SOMEWHERE

Another routine changer—change your location. In his book *A New Kind of Christian*, Brian McLaren says this:

"I look back over my years in ministry and ask what has really helped people change and deepen spiritually: (1) youth retreats, (2) short-term mission trips, (3) some small groups . . . (4) many one-to-one relationships, (5) getting people involved leading something or serving somewhere. I look over this list and wonder what they have in common. The biggest thing—intensity. Odd: we try to make our spiritual formation experiences routine, and that maybe guarantees they become less effective. The more intense and less routine the educational experience, the greater the impact."[6]

While I might not agree with everything McLaren says, I think he's got a point here. In fact, I have a little formula: change of pace + change of place = change of perspective.

A change of pace typically means slowing down to find opportunities to stop in the middle of the chaotic and frenetic pace of our lives. Change of place means changing our latitude or our altitude. Jesus practiced this often. Consider the following:

"Very early in the morning, while it was still dark, He got up, went out, and made His way to a deserted place. And He was praying there" (Mark 1:35).

"Yet He often withdrew to deserted places and prayed" (Luke 5:16).

Or how about Exodus 33:7-11? In this passage, we see Moses moving outside of his daily leadership routine. He set up a tent outside the camp in which he could spend time with God.

You have to disrupt your routine so you can think new thoughts. New environments stimulate new ideas. One of the best ways to change your pace, place, and perspective is to go on a mission trip. Few experiences will transform you further into Christ's likeness like a short-term experience on the mission field.

What opportunities do you have in the next six months to go on a trip that would change your latitude and altitude?

Listen to Part I of an audio conversation called "Chasing the Goose in D.C." This roundtable recording was made by some original members of National Community Church where author Mark Batterson pastors. It's real people remembering a time in their lives when they chased the Goose together. Your leader will e-mail it to you this week, or you can find it as a podcast at *threadsmedia. com/chase-the-goose.*

TAKE OFF YOUR SANDALS

Let me share one of my fundamental convictions: There are people who would say they've never experienced a miracle. I would suggest that we are surrounded by miracles.

I think a fundamental dimension of spiritual growth is learning to recognize and appreciate the miracles that are all around you all the time. Did you know that this very second there are approximately six trillion reactions taking place in every cell of your body? Your heart will pump about 100,000 times today without skipping a beat, you will inhale and exhale 23,000 times. Your body is doing a hundred different things right now that you pay no attention to: digesting, reproducing new cells, purifying toxins, maintaining hormonal balance, converting stored energy from fat to blood sugar, and repairing damaged cells. Those are just a few of them. When was the last time you thanked God for any of that stuff?

Think about it—it's in our nature to take stuff for granted. The "problem" with God is that He's so constant. And He's so good at what He does—unconditional love, new mercies every morning, the sun coming up and going down, the common grace that allows us to open our eyes—He's so good, so constantly and so consistently, that we take Him for granted.

Albert Einstein said, "There are two ways to live: you can live as if nothing is a miracle; you can live as if everything is a miracle."[7] A poet by the name of Elizabeth Barrett Browning said it this way: "Earth's crammed with heaven, and every common bush afire with God; but only he who sees, takes off his shoes, the rest sit round it and pluck blackberries."[8]

Make a list of 10 miracles you experienced during the last week.

In the Old Testament, taking off one's shoes was a sign of great respect for another.

Let me make one last observation from Moses' encounter with God. The last verse says: "Take your sandals off your feet" (Exodus 3:5). What a fascinating command. *Take off your sandals.* Most of us have heard or read this story so many times that the obvious eludes us—the holy ground wasn't the promised land. The holy ground was right where Moses was standing.

I think many of us live our lives saying, "When I get to the promised land, you better believe I'm going to take off my sandals." I think God reminded Moses that the holy ground is right here, right now. Given that, take off your sandals. Celebrate who God is. Celebrate what God is doing. Right now.

The Wild Goose chase isn't just about getting to a particular destination, it's about enjoying the journey—the spiritual adventure we're on. It's about living in the moment day in and day out. It's about seeing the miracles that are all around us all the time. It's about saying to God, "Here I am." It's about taking off our sandals and worshiping God right here and right now. It's about a moment-by-moment sensitivity to the Holy Spirit that literally turns every day into a spiritual adventure.

NOW WHAT?

PRAYER

Lord help us. Help us. Many of us feel like we are a long way away from the spiritual adventure that You ordained for us. Many of us have no emotional energy left to even think about adventure or chasing the Wild Goose. God I pray that You would save us from our boredom. Let us be a people who live by faith so that we experience a holy rush of adrenaline coming from obeying You. Help us disrupt the routine where it needs to be disrupted and make some small changes in our lives this week that would make a huge difference in our routines.

Lord I pray that we would be a people who learn to take off our sandals and see You. Would you once again invade the reality of our lives and turn them into what You originally intended them to be? Give us patience, let us enjoy the journey and not get too frustrated or too discouraged. We offer ourselves to you. Here we are. In Jesus' name, amen.

SCRIPTURE MEMORY

"'This will take place,' He continued, 'so they will believe that the LORD, the God of their fathers, the God of Abraham, the God of Isaac, and the God of Jacob, has appeared to you'" (Exodus 4:5).

CHASING THE GOOSE

• Watch *The Ten Commandments.*
• Google "Elizabeth Barrett Browning" and read some of her poems.
• Disrupt your routine by planning a fast, changing your Bible translation, changing the location of your devotion time, or starting to journal.

notes

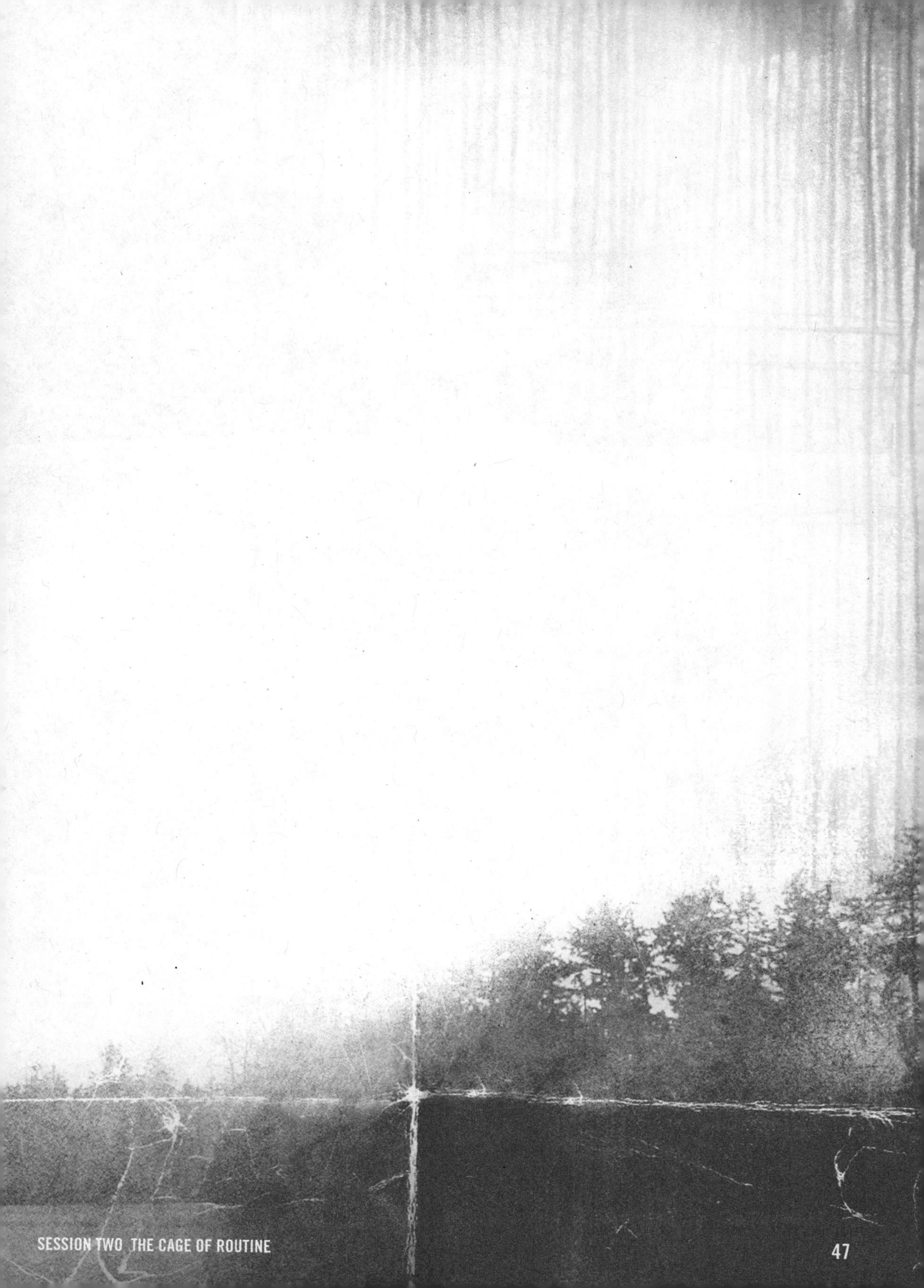

SESSION THREE CHASE THE GOOSE

THE CAGE OF
ASSUMPTIONS

WE MISS THE ADVENTURE OF CHASING THE WILD GOOSE WHEN WE TRUST OUR ASSUMPTIONS MORE THAN WE TRUST GOD. As we age, many of us stop believing and start assuming. We stop living out of right-brain imagination and we start living out of left-brain memory. And we put eight-foot ceilings on what God can do.

One of our kids' favorite destinations in D.C. is the National Air and Space Museum. It's not too far from our home, so our family loves to venture over there to retrace the history of aviation—from kites to rockets. When my youngest child Josiah was just a toddler, we visited an exhibit of a cross-section of an American Airlines Douglas DC-7 airplane. As we approached the display to walk through it, I noticed a look of concern on Josiah's face. I asked him if he wanted to get on the airplane, and, in that cute little toddler voice, Josiah asked, "It not take off?"

Lora and I couldn't help but laugh at the impossibility. There was no engine, no wings, no runway . . . it was just a 20-foot cross-section of an airplane. Yet Josiah thought there was a possibility, however remote, that the thing might just take off. That epitomizes the beauty of childhood.

In general, those who are left-brain oriented are more logical, rational, and analytical. Right-brained folks tend to be more random, intuitive, and imagination-ruled.

GROWING UP IS HARD TO DO

Children don't know what can't be done. They have not yet defined what is and what is not possible. No impossibilities; no assumptions. The only limitation they know is their God-given imagination.

Unfortunately, we grow up, and tragic things happen to most of us in that process. Memory overtakes imagination; we stop make-believing, and we start making assumptions. We start thinking the way we've always thought, we start doing what we've always done, and generally speaking, the older we get, the more assumptions we make. Before we know it, we've lost our sense of adventure, and most tragically, that loss of adventure invades our spirituality. Pretty soon, our faith has no edge to it, and we end up in the cage of assumptions. In order to break free, we need to come to a place where imagination overtakes memory.

> In what areas of life have you stopped make-believing and started assuming?

> Are any assumptions good assumptions? If so, what are they? If not, why not?

If you visit Washington, D.C., make sure to drop by the National Air and Space Museum. Check out the Moon rock, the Wright Flyer, and the Einstein Planetarium.

> What would it look like for imagination to overtake memory in your life?

EIGHT-FOOT CEILINGS

One year, I took my sons Parker and Josiah camping to celebrate Parker's birthday. It was a cool, fall night with a slight chill in the air, and there were no city lights to compete with the clear sky. When the sun went down and the stars came out, we headed to an open field behind our campsite, lay on our backs with our heads just a few inches apart, and gazed up into the heavens. We only stayed there for a few minutes, but it seemed like an eternity. Parker pointed out some constellations that he knew. Josiah discovered "moving stars," otherwise known as airplanes. As we looked into the sky that literally stretched billions of light years in every direction, we were reminded of how big our God is. Looking into the night sky recalibrates me spiritually. It reminds me of how small I am and how big God is. That's a healthy and holy thing for me.

Looking at the night sky was also a holy experience for Abraham. Abraham's recognition of the expanse of God's creation initiated his breaking free from the cage of assumptions:

"After these events, the word of the LORD came to Abram in a vision: 'Do not be afraid, Abram. I am your shield; your reward will be very great.' But Abram said, 'Lord GOD, what can You give me, since I am childless and the heir of my house is Eliezer of Damascus?' Abram continued, 'Look, You have given me no offspring, so a slave born in my house will be my heir.' Now the word of the LORD came to him: 'This one will not be your heir; instead, one who comes from your own body will be your heir.' He took him outside and said, 'Look at the sky and count the stars, if you are able to count them.' Then He said to him, 'Your offspring will be that numerous.' Abram believed the LORD, and He credited it to him as righteousness" (Genesis 15:1-6).

Let me give you some background. Abraham and Sarah were childless. Their deepest desire was to be parents, but Sarah was barren and they lived with that pain for decades. In their culture, having no children also meant they had to live with a profound sense of shame. I imagine Sarah felt a familiar knot in the pit of her soul every time she heard the news from a friend: "I'm pregnant." I think she felt the pain on hearing the laugh of a child. I'm sure she and Abraham must have cried together. I bet they had a few fights about it. They felt the ache of emptiness and the confusion of helplessness because they could not have what they wanted most. And my guess is that it never got easier over time.

But one day God made a promise: "Take a look at the sky and start counting the stars, if you can. That's how many descendants you will have." But it's not just what God said; it's what He did that's worth noting here. If you look at this passage very carefully, you'll notice that God took Abraham *outside*. I think it's easy to read a passage like this and read right past one of the most significant points.

Imagine the scene. Abraham was holed up in his tent. In a sense, he had a man-made, eight-foot ceiling over his head. Then God decided to take him on a little field trip outside of that manufactured environment. He told Abraham to look up into the night sky and to count the stars.

In Genesis 12, God introduced Himself to Abraham. It was in that passage that God called Abraham to go to somewhere new and different, and promised him that Abraham would be the father of many nations.

Giving birth to children was considered a religious and patriotic obligation and privilege by the Jewish people. Barrenness was viewed as the most severe punishment against a female that God could give. It is interesting to note, however, that the mothers of the Jewish race—Sarah, Rebekah, and Rachel—all experienced difficulty in having children.

I have no idea how long it took—it might have been an all-nighter. Abraham must have lost count of the number of times he lost count of the stars, but by the time he was done, he had learned an important object lesson he would never forget. Abraham would never look into the sky the same way again because the stars in the sky were a nightly reminder of the promise God had made to him.

So why did God take Abraham outside? Why did He tell him to look into the night sky? Why did He tell him to count the stars? I think the answer is so obvious it eludes us. As long as Abraham was inside his tent, his vision was obscured by an eight-foot ceiling. That ceiling kept the promises of God out of sight. And as the old adage goes, "Out of sight, out of mind." I think God wanted to remind Abraham of how big He was, so He told Abraham to go outside and do a little stargazing. I think it was God's way of saying, "Abraham, don't put an eight-foot ceiling on what I can do."

> Write down three promises of God from Scripture you need to pull into sight.

> List areas of your life that might be limited by an eight-foot ceiling.

> For each area, write down one practical thing you can do to remind yourself how big God is.

BIG "G" GOD

It was about half a century ago that one of my favorite writers, A. W. Tozer, said, "The low view of God entertained almost universally among Christians is the cause of a hundred lesser evils everywhere among us.

The number of stars visible to the naked eye on any given night depends on several variables, including light pollution, atmospheric turbulence, and cloud cover, but astronomers estimate that there are 100 billion stars in our galaxy, the Milky Way. One estimate of the number of stars ranges from 10^{22} to 10^{24}.

Aiden Wilson Tozer wrote the Christian classics *The Pursuit of God* and *The Knowledge of the Holy*. Prayer was central to his ministry, and his biographer, James L. Snyder, said, "His preaching and his writings were but extensions of his prayer life." His epitaph reads, "A. W. Tozer—A Man of God."[10]

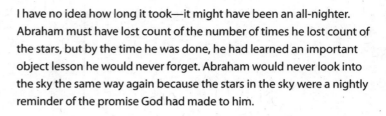

. . . [But] the man who comes to a right belief about God is relieved of ten thousand temporal problems."[9]

Many of us end up in the cage of assumptions and miss the spiritual adventure because we reduce God to the size of our biggest problem. Or we reduce Him to the extent of our left-brain logic and whatever can fit within the cerebral cortex. Or we reduce Him to the size of our greatest fear or our worst sin. When we do this, we end up with a god—a small "g" god—that looks an awful lot like us and seems to be about our size. As the saying goes, "God made man in His image, and man has been returning the favor ever since." This is idolatry in its most subtle, yet deadly, form. I'm convinced our biggest problem is not really our biggest problem. Our biggest problem is that we don't think God is bigger than our biggest problem.

> What is the biggest problem you are facing right now? How does your view of God compare to your view of the problem?

> It has been said that "God made man in His image, and man has been returning the favor ever since." Do you agree or disagree with that statement? Why? How is that idolatry?

Spiritual growth is about so much more than learning new things. It's not just about head knowledge; it's about knowledge becoming a conviction, and that conviction actually dictating the way we live our lives. It's not just about information; it's about a belief that actually transforms our lives. I'd rather know one person with one deeply held conviction than one thousand people who know one thousand things.

Isaiah 55:8-9 has become my theological linchpin. It is the starting place for the way I think about God and the way I relate to Him:

"'For My thoughts are not your thoughts, and your ways are not My ways.' This is the Lord's declaration. 'For as heaven is higher than earth, so My ways are higher than your ways, and My thoughts than your thoughts.'"

For a challenging book about the way we view God, check out *Your God Is Too Small* by J. B. Phillips.

Isaiah was an 8th-century B.C. prophet whose message was one of both judgment and grace. He prophesied about the imminent fall of Judah but also about the return of the nation to the Lord and the coming of the Messiah.

Listen to Part II of the audio conversation between the young adults of NCC: "Chasing the Goose in D.C." Your leader will e-mail it to you this week, or you can find it as a podcast at *threadsmedia.com/chase-the-goose.*

Three of the four passages to the left were written by Paul. Considering that Paul, in the course of his life, saw the gospel stretch from a handful of followers in Jerusalem to the entire known world, it's no wonder he had such a high view of the capability of God.

Light travels at the speed of 186,000 miles per second. In the time it takes me to snap my fingers, light circumnavigates the globe about half a dozen times. That's faster than fast. Let me try to put it in perspective. Our sun is about 93 million miles away. If I were to drive a car 65 miles per hour, for 24 hours a day, for 365 days a year—no pit stops, no rest stops, no gas stops—it would take me more than 163 years to get there. But the light that warms my face on a sunny day is only 8 minutes old because light travels that fast.

The sun is the nearest star in our tiny little galaxy called the Milky Way, but astrophysicists have discovered galaxies at least 13.7 billion light years away. One light year is equivalent to 5.88 trillion miles, so the farthest galaxy is 13.7 billion times 5.88 trillion. That means God created galaxies about 80 sextillion miles away from us. The distance is virtually incomprehensible.

According to God, that's about the distance between your thoughts and His thoughts.

So here's my thought: our best thoughts on our best days are about 13.7 billion light years short of how good and how great God really is. We underestimate God by 13.7 billion light years. He is 13.7 billion light years beyond our wildest imaginations while we live in our tiny cages of assumptions.

When you enter into a relationship with Christ and you begin to chase the Wild Goose, all assumptions are out the window. Why? Because God exists outside of space-time dimensions. He is omniscient, omnipotent, and omnipresent. Consider these verses:

"I am able to do all things through Him who strengthens me" (Philippians 4:13).

"Now to Him who is able to do above and beyond all that we ask or think—according to the power that works in you—to Him be glory in the church and in Christ Jesus to all generations, forever and ever. Amen" (Ephesians 3:20-21).

"If God is for us, who is against us?" (Romans 8:31).

"Everything is possible to the one who believes" (Mark 9:23).

When you enter into relationship with God, He takes the eight-foot ceiling off of your life; that's the heart of the story of Abraham. He told

Abraham to look up in the sky: "Look at the stars. I'm the One who made them. Do not put an eight-foot ceiling on what I can do." Quit assuming. Start believing.

And that's exactly what Abraham did.

> In what area of your life do you need to quit assuming and start believing? What does that look like, practically?

DEALING WITH DOUBT

Did Abraham ever doubt? Of course. He went through moments of frustration and experienced fear. But Romans 4:18-21 captures the essence of his faith:

"Against hope, with hope he believed, so that he became the father of many nations, according to what had been spoken: So will your descendants be. He considered his own body to be already dead (since he was about a hundred years old), and the deadness of Sarah's womb, without weakening in the faith. He did not waver in unbelief at God's promise, but was strengthened in his faith and gave glory to God, because he was fully convinced that what He had promised He was also able to perform."

> What do you think this verse means when it says that Abraham was "fully convinced"? What caused Abraham to become fully convinced?

> Are you fully convinced that God has the power to do what He promised in your life? Why or why not? What has led you to that decision?

> What promises of God have you given up on?

Romans 4 is Paul's biographical case study of Abraham. In that chapter, Paul held up Abraham as the enduring example of saving faith.

To break free from the cage of assumptions, we have to develop our faith. Faith isn't logical, but it isn't illogical either. Faith is *theo*-logical. It adds God into the equation so that what we're able to imagine isn't determined solely by our human ability. Abraham faced the facts; he wasn't out of touch with reality. But he was also fully persuaded that God had the power to deliver on His promises.

F. B. Meyer said, "Unbelief puts circumstances between itself and Christ, so as not to see Him . . . Faith puts Christ between itself and circumstances."[11]

Where is God compared to you and your circumstances right now? Mark His presence in the illustration below.

Circumstances

Circumstances   You   Circumstances

Circumstances

Let me repeat myself: Faith is not mindless ignorance; it simply refuses to limit God to the logical constraints of the left brain. Faith puts God between us and our circumstances. So, let's get personal for a moment. This isn't just about a guy named Abraham who lived thousands of years ago; it's about you and me.

Let's talk about a couple of assumptions that tend to keep us from chasing the Wild Goose and living the spiritual adventure God ordained for our lives.

I'M TOO OLD

Here's an assumption: Ninety-year-old women don't have babies. Pretty fair statement, right? It is a biological impossibility for a barren, post-menopausal woman to get pregnant. Or is it? Can I give you some good news? One of the core values at NCC is that it's never too late to become who you might have been. God is the God of second chances. You may feel like time has passed you by and the window of opportunity closed a long time ago. But the good news is that it's never too late.

At your small group meeting time this week, watch the teaching video "Breaking Out of Assumptions." You'll see author Mark Batterson discuss the eight-foot ceilings of our lives and how our vision of God can break through them.

After my book, *In a Pit with a Lion on a Snowy Day*, was published, I started hearing stories about people who were quitting jobs to chase lions, and some of them stirred my spirit in ways I can't even describe. Surprisingly, the most inspiring stories I received were from people who were not the target audience for the book. These people weren't young adults; instead, they were people in their 60s, 70s, and 80s. I love the fact that these people figured out they are old—not dead—and they still have lions to chase. If you're still breathing, God has more for you, and the Wild Goose still wants to take you on a spiritual adventure.

Caleb, one of the original 12 spies who Moses sent into the promised land, was 85 when he finally arrived. As Joshua divided up the land, Caleb said, "I am still as strong today as I was the day Moses sent me out. My strength for battle and for daily tasks is now as it was then" (Joshua 14:11). He was 85 years old, but lived with the attitude that said, "Bring on the promised land because I'm going to take it." And Caleb's not alone.

Jesus was 30 years old when He transitioned His career from carpentry to ministry.

Moses was in his 80s when he led the Israelites out of Egypt.

Noah was in his 500s when he built the ark.

You are never too old to go on a Wild Goose chase.

Can you think of other people in the Bible who seemed too old to do what God called them to do?

Write down the name of someone you know who believes they're too old to pursue something big. What can you do to encourage him or her to break free from this cage of assumption and chase the Wild Goose? (And if you are that person, what is one practical thing you will do this week to break free from this cage?)

In a Pit with a Lion on a Snowy Day is based on the account of Benaiah from 2 Samuel 23:20. To read more or to order the Bible study version, *Chase the Lion*, visit *threadsmedia.com*.

Read Caleb's story in Joshua 14:6-14.

I'M TOO YOUNG

Let's flip the coin and consider another common assumption: I'm too young. It just seems like God uses a lot of really old people and really young people. Most scholars think Mary was probably a teenager when she became the mother of God. What a huge responsibility! The disciples were most likely 20-somethings. David was just a kid when he took on Goliath.

In 1 Timothy 4:12, Paul encouraged the young pastor Timothy:

"No one should despise your youth; instead, you should be an example to the believers in speech, in conduct, in love, in faith, in purity."

Paul didn't just tell Timothy to be simply good in certain areas or do the best he could; he told Timothy to set an example. To be a role model. To be a leader worth following.

Paul encouraged Timothy to be an example in five areas—teaching, living, loving, demonstrating faith, and practicing purity.

In which of these areas are you setting a good example for other believers, young and old?

In which areas do you need to set a better example?

You are never too old to be used by God. And you are never too young to be used by God.

"I'm not ready," another assumption, is closely related to "I'm too young." Here's the reality: You'll never be experienced enough, educated enough, or spiritual enough. Does that cover all of us? Too often we allow what we cannot do to keep us from doing what we can, and we allow who we are not to keep us from being who we can be. I think we allow the fear of failure to keep us from even trying, or we allow the fear of looking foolish to keep us from daring to be different.

Timothy was a native of Lystra. Paul and Barnabas went there during the first missionary journey, and legend has it that they stayed in Timothy's home. Timothy was the child of a Jewish mother and Greek father, and he accompanied Paul on many of his later travels.

A lot of us forfeit the miracle because we are afraid of looking foolish or we are afraid of falling on our faces. We never accomplish anything because we never try anything.

Can you think of other people in the Bible who were too young or unprepared to do what God called them to do? Who are they?

Write down the name of someone you know who believes he or she is too young or not ready to pursue something big. What can you do to encourage this person to break free from the cage of assumption and chase the Wild Goose? (If you are allowing assumptions to hold you back, what is one practical thing you will do this week to break free from this cage?)

IT'S NEVER BEEN DONE THAT WAY BEFORE

Until the late 1960s, the standard high-jumping technique consisted of leaping over the bar by straddling it face down. This technique was called the western roll. The world record was about seven and a half feet. Then came Dick Fosbury. Instead of straddling the bar sideways, Fosbury jumped over the bar shoulders first and twisted so that he would face up instead of face down. The coach tried to get him to either drop his unorthodox style or quit the sport, but Fosbury kept perfecting his style.

You can check out footage of the famous Fosbury flop on *youtube.com.*

The 1968 Olympic Games proved to be a turning point in the history of the high jump. Fosbury walked into the Mexico City Olympic arena not only as a new name to the sport, but with a new approach that would revolutionize the sport. His style looked strange and awkward to many and was unsettling to his opponents.

The crowd initially viewed him as a novelty but his continued success at clearing the ever-increasing height soon made it apparent he was a serious contender. Valentin Gavrilov from the Soviet Union failed at his attempt of 2.22 meters while Fosbury and his U. S. teammate, Edward Caruthers, cleared their way to a jump-off. The bar was set at 2.24 meters. Caruthers failed. Fosbury took his new style of high jump over the bar and into the history books, and Fosbury jumped away with a gold medal win and a new Olympic record. Within a few years, the Fosbury flop became the standard method of jumping.[12]

Progress in every cultural arena depends upon those who are willing to challenge the assumptions. Amazon did not assume you needed a bookstore to sell books. Wikipedia decided you don't need door-to-door encyclopedia salesmen; they even decided you don't need books or experts! Fosbury assumed you don't have to go over forward; you can go over backward, and you may even win a gold medal and set a world record by doing so.

Why were the Pharisees so threatened by Jesus? Why were they so resistant to His ministry? Because He challenged every assumption in the book!

Have you ever heard anyone say, "It's never been done that way before"? I think that's another assumption keeping us in the cage. As I look at my own Wild Goose chase, I think the defining moments are the moments when my assumptions were challenged and I had a choice to make—hang on to my assumptions or hang on to God. I can't do both.

I think the church needs to challenge assumptions. What if we believed there are ways of doing church that no one has thought of yet? Are there ways of sharing our faith and reaching people far from God that we haven't dreamed of yet? Are there ways of discipling people that we have not imagined?

What assumptions does your faith community need to challenge?

Are there dangers to challenging assumptions? Why or why not? What is the appropriate way of challenging assumptions?

Listen to "Revolutionaries" by Bethany Dillon on the *Chase the Goose* playlist. Your leader will send you the whole playlist via e-mail, or you can find it at *threadsmedia.com/chase-the-goose*. Use these songs as the background music for your study.

What are some other assumptions people make that keep them from chasing the Wild Goose? What are some other assumptions you've made that have kept you from chasing the Wild Goose?

THE LAST LAUGH

I want to give a closing picture of what happened in Abraham's and Sarah's lives. I think the older we get, the more assumptions we tend to make. But that wasn't the case with Abraham. As he got older, he made fewer assumptions; instead he demonstrated more faith.

I wish I could tell you God always delivers on His promise in one week or one month or one year. Abraham was about 75 years old when God called him out of Ur, and that's when the Wild Goose chase began for him. Then 25 years later, when Abraham was 100 years old, God fulfilled His promise.

"The LORD came to Sarah as He had said, and the LORD did for Sarah what He had promised. Sarah became pregnant and bore a son to Abraham in his old age, at the appointed time God had told him. Abraham named his son who was born to him—the one Sarah bore to him—Isaac. When his son Isaac was eight days old, Abraham circumcised him, as God had commanded him. Abraham was 100 years old when his son Isaac was born to him. Sarah said, 'God has made me laugh, and everyone who hears will laugh with me'" (Genesis 21:1-6).

I don't think we can comprehend the depth of emotion Sarah must have felt as she said these words. Waiting 25 years for God to fulfill His promise must have seemed like an eternity to Abraham and Sarah, and it had to be spiritually confusing and emotionally exhausting.

As the years passed, Abraham and Sarah must have lost a little bit of their laughter. It's hard to laugh when you feel a deep sadness in your soul that never goes away. That's why Isaac's name is so apropos—it means "laughter." I used to think that the name was punishment because Sarah laughed at God when God said she was going to have a baby, but I've changed my mind. A child's laughter is precious. Nothing brings me greater joy than hearing my kids laugh.

Ur is located between the modern-day city of Baghdad, Iraq, and the head of the Persian Gulf. It is often called "Ur of the Chaldeans" in biblical texts to refer to the Chaldeans, who settled the area in 900 B.C.

God's promise that Abraham would be the father of many nations was eventually fulfilled in Christ. According to the New Testament, all those who have faith in Christ become children of Abraham, who demonstrated that kind of faith.

God is no different. God loves it when we laugh, and I think Isaac was God's way of giving Abraham and Sarah their laughter back. He is the God who literally conceives laughter.

I also think Isaac's name reveals a dimension of God's character. When Sarah laughed at God, God said, "Is anything impossible for the LORD?" (Genesis 18:14). A part of me wonders if God waited 25 years until the thought of Sarah having a baby was absolutely inconceivable (pun intended). Then He broke through the eight-foot ceiling and proved once again that nothing is impossible for Him. Isaac was God's way of saying to Abraham and Sarah, "I'm going to have the last laugh."

Is there an area of life where you have lost your laughter? Why? How do you think you can get it back?

What eight-foot ceilings do you need God to remove in your life? Write out a prayer asking God to help you see beyond that ceiling.

NOW WHAT?

PRAYER

Lord, thank You that You are the God who is so much bigger than our problems, fears, failures, and assumptions. As the heavens are higher than the earth, so are Your ways and Your thoughts higher than our ways and our thoughts. May we look up into that sky, do a little bit of stargazing of our own, and remind ourselves once again of how big You are. Coax us out of this tiny little cage of assumptions that we find ourselves in.

May we have the courage to live by faith, to chase after the Wild Goose. God help us not to become captive to these assumptions that we've made—too old or too young, not educated enough, not experienced enough, not spiritual enough, it's never been done that way before. Help us to open ourselves up and say to You, "Have Your will and Your way in our lives, for there is nothing that You cannot do." We are grateful because we dwell in possibilities. All things are possible for those who believe. We celebrate who You are and what that means in our lives. In Jesus' name, amen.

SCRIPTURE MEMORY

"'For My thoughts are not your thoughts, and your ways are not My ways.' This is the LORD's declaration. 'For as heaven is higher than earth, so My ways are higher than your ways, and My thoughts than your thoughts'" (Isaiah 55:8-9).

CHASING THE GOOSE

• Watch *Rudy*.
• Read *Created to Be God's Friend* by Henry Blackaby.
• Go stargazing and learn a few constellations.

notes

THE CAGE OF
GUILT

THE ENEMY'S TACTICS HAVEN'T CHANGED SINCE THE GARDEN OF EDEN.
He's still trying to neutralize us spiritually by getting us to focus on what we've
done wrong in the past. Satan uses guilt to turn us into reactionaries. Jesus
came to recondition our spiritual reflexes and turn us into revolutionaries for
His cause. As long as we're focused on what we've done wrong in the past,
we won't have the energy left to dream the kind of dreams God has in mind
for us.

If you're anything like me, you love success stories. They motivate me and
inspire me. But to be honest, every once in awhile I like to hear a good old-
fashioned failure story. You know, the kind that makes you feel better because
it reminds you that life could be worse. I'm joking, but in some ways seeing
failure in others is helpful to me because I'm reminded that I'm not alone.
I guess I need to know I'm not the only one who wrestles with doubt and
whose life is entangled in sins. That's why I love Peter.

SUCCESS STORIES

When I start to feel badly about myself, I just think about Peter, a disciple who was used so powerfully by God despite the many mistakes he made along the way. I think we can draw encouragement and learn some lessons from his life.

> Can you think of some other Bible stories of people who failed miserably but were still used powerfully by God? List three and the lessons you can learn from them.

> How do you define "success"? How about "failure"? How do you think God defines them?

In Luke 22:31-34, Jesus prophesied about the events that would occur later that night. He said:

"'Simon, Simon, look out! Satan has asked to sift you like wheat. But I have prayed for you that your faith may not fail. And you, when you have turned back, strengthen your brothers.'

'Lord,' he told Him, 'I'm ready to go with You both to prison and to death!'

'I tell you, Peter,' He said, 'the rooster will not crow today until you deny three times that you know Me!'"

You've got to love Peter's bravado. He had no idea what was about to happen, but he very boldly declared his loyalty to Jesus—even to death.

> Has there ever been a time in your life when you blindly and boldly devoted yourself to something or someone only to chicken out later? If so, when was it? Why did you chicken out?

"[The devil] was a murderer from the beginning and has not stood in the truth, because there is no truth in him. When he tells a lie, he speaks from his own nature, because he is a liar and the father of liars" (John 8:44).

Peter has the reputation of being passionate, impetuous, and hot-headed, characteristics that worked against him in some cases, but also served to make him a great leader. After the resurrection, Peter became the leader of the disciples and the foundation of the church in Jerusalem.

In this interaction with Peter, Jesus called him by his old name, "Simon." It is possible that this signifies Peter would soon act according to his old nature.

CONDITIONED REFLEXES

In the study *Chase the Lion*, we talked about the impact that conditioned reflexes have on the way we approach fear and failure. Those same conditioned reflexes also serve as catalysts to keep us bound in the cage of guilt. Here's how it works.

During the late 1800s and early 1900s, a Russian physiologist and physician named Ivan Pavlov published some groundbreaking studies that won him a Nobel Prize. He recognized that dogs naturally salivated to food, but he wanted to see if he could trigger the salivation in response to another stimulus. As you may recall from high school science class, Pavlov conditioned the dogs by ringing a bell and then feeding them their food. Eventually, the dogs began to salivate upon hearing the ringing bell regardless of whether they were simultaneously brought food or not. Pavlov referred to this learned relationship as a conditioned reflex.[13]

I experienced a conditioned reflex recently when I went to Delaware to compete in the Dewey Beach Triathlon. A little doughnut shop called the Fractured Prune can be found there. If you don't get to try one on this side of heaven, don't worry. I'm pretty sure the marriage supper of the Lamb will feature Fractured Prune doughnuts. As I drove to Dewey Beach, I began salivating just thinking about them. But just in case you haven't been to the Fractured Prune, think about Cinnabon. Who doesn't start salivating when they smell a Cinnabon? It seems like there is a Cinnabon in every airport. You step off that plane, take one good whiff of the airport air, and immediately begin to salivate.

To one degree or another, all of us are Pavlovian. We've been consciously or subconsciously conditioned by different stimuli over the course of our entire lives, and much of our behavior is dictated by those conditioned reflexes. Here's another example from my life: Every time I fill up my gas tank, I instinctively look in the side-view mirror before driving off. Why? Because a few years ago, I didn't check to make sure I had removed the gas hose from my tank, and I ripped the hose right out of the gas pump when I drove away. That one incident conditioned me to glance in my mirror every time I pull away from a gas station.

Over the course of our lifetimes, we acquire an elaborate repertoire of conditioned reflexes. Some of them are minor idiosyncrasies like a nervous laugh, a half-smile, or a twitch. Others become major personality traits. I think a critical personality is often born out of psychological insecurity. We criticize in others what we don't like about ourselves. While most conditioned reflexes are normal and fairly

Ivan Pavlov was the son of the village priest in Ryazan, Russia. Pavlov enrolled in seminary to pursue theological studies but switched to the sciences after reading Charles Darwin's *On the Origin of the Species*.

When you get a second, check out *fracturedprune.com* . . . if you think you can handle it.

benign, others are extremely destructive. Big or small, conscious or subconscious, harmless or harmful, one thing is certain—we are far more conditioned than we realize.

What are some conditioned reflexes in your life? How did they become conditioned reflexes?

Are your conditioned reflexes benign or harmful? Why?

I would submit that part of spiritual growth is recognizing how we've been conditioned and allowing God to recondition our reflexes. That was a major focus of Jesus' preaching ministry. How many times did He say, "You have heard it said . . . but I tell you . . ."? He was reconditioning His listeners. When Jesus told His followers to turn the other cheek and love their enemies, He was reconditioning their emotions. When He told them to give to whomever asked of them and not to turn anyone away in need, He was reconditioning their wallets. When He told them to pray for the very ones persecuting them, He was reconditioning their values.

There are tremendous principles we can draw from Pavlov's research as we talk about guilt and how it keeps us from living the spiritual adventure of the Wild Goose chase. When we sin, guilt is a healthy and a holy reflex. We should thank God for the conviction of the Wild Goose. He loves us enough to prevent us from hurting ourselves. So He convicts us, or prompts us, in such a way that we know what we are about to do or have done is wrong and will eventually turn us into people we don't want to be. Thank God for the guilt that comes from Holy Spirit conviction.

But some conditioned reflexes of false guilt become like psychological straitjackets that immobilize us emotionally, relationally, or spiritually. The moment we acknowledge the conviction of the Holy Spirit, and confess our sin to God, our sin is forgiven and forgotten. Isn't that an amazing thing? When was the last time you said, "God, thank You that Your grace is enough and Your grace is sufficient"? For most of us, it's far easier for us to accept God's forgiveness than it is for us to forgive ourselves. Why? Because we can forgive but we can't

For a session of reconditioning, read Matthew 5–7. The Sermon on the Mount contains the record of Jesus reconditioning the reflexes of His earliest followers, and it is applicable for us today as well.

forget. If we don't allow the grace of God to completely saturate and sanctify our sinful memory, many of us will continue to experience false guilt over confessed sin, resulting in spiritual paralysis. We run the risk of becoming so fixated on past mistakes that we forfeit future opportunities. We mistakenly think our sins disqualify us from God using us, and our feelings of guilt become the cage that keeps us from chasing the Wild Goose.

What's the difference between good guilt and bad guilt?

Describe times when you experienced both good and bad guilt. What was the result of each?

"Faith is ... the character of accepting acceptance."[14]
–Paul Tillich

What sins are you having trouble forgetting? Why do you think it's difficult for you to forget them? Do you feel like God has forgotten them? Why or why not?

CAGE OF GUILT

Let's look back at Peter to see how he landed in the cage of guilt:

"They seized Him, led Him away, and brought Him into the high priest's house. Meanwhile Peter was following at a distance. They lit a fire in the middle of the courtyard and sat down together, and Peter sat among them" (Luke 22:54-55).

Now I want to make an observation here. We always give Peter a hard time for being the guy who denied Jesus, right? But where were the other disciples? At least Peter followed at a distance. None of the others got close enough to get caught. So let's give some props to Peter for at least getting close enough to be in a situation where he could deny Jesus.

"When a servant saw him sitting in the firelight, and looked closely at him, she said, 'This man was with Him too.' But he denied it: 'Woman, I don't know Him!'" (Luke 22:56-57).

You would think Peter's memory would trigger right here and he would remember what Jesus said earlier.

"After a little while, someone else saw him and said, 'You're one of them too!' 'Man, I am not!' Peter said" (Luke 22:58).

Alright, if I was Peter, I would be thinking, *That's two strikes. I'm not going to get the third one.*

"About an hour later, another kept insisting, 'This man was certainly with Him, since he's also a Galilean.' But Peter said, 'Man I don't know what you're talking about!' Immediately, while he was still speaking, a rooster crowed. Then the Lord turned and looked at Peter. So Peter remembered the word of the Lord, how He had said to him, 'Before the rooster crows today, you will deny Me three times.' And he went outside and wept bitterly" (Luke 22:59-62).

Should Peter get any "extra credit" for at least following closely behind Jesus? Why or why not?

Do you think that in the moment Peter realized he had denied Christ? Why do you think he did it again? Can you relate to Peter in that?

Peter's denial is also recorded in Matthew 26, Mark 14, and John 18. Matthew points out that Peter's accent betrayed him. John notes that the relative of the man he attacked in the garden of Gethsemane recognized him.

Looking at Scripture through the lens of Ivan Pavlov is an interesting exercise, and Peter makes an interesting case study. I have read this story countless times, but a few years ago I had a thought that changed the way I viewed the story. I wonder if from that moment on Peter felt a twinge of guilt every time he heard a rooster crow.

Have you noticed the way different stimuli trigger different memories? Seemingly insignificant sights, sounds, and smells can evoke powerful memories. Whenever I hear "You Got It" by Roy Orbison, I'm transported mentally and emotionally right back to Lakeshore

Drive, driving from the University of Chicago in downtown Chicago with Lora when we were dating. It was our song. One whiff of lilac and I'm transported through time and space to my grandma's backyard. I wonder if a rooster's crow had a similar but negative psychological effect on Peter. He let Jesus down when Jesus needed him the most, and I've got to think that sound triggered something in his auditory cortex that produced a Pavlovian effect on Peter. Every time a rooster crowed, it put Peter right back in the cage of guilt.

We don't have a lot of roosters in Washington, D.C. There are plenty of car alarms and police sirens, but no roosters. When our mission team was on the Galápagos Islands, I'll never forget waking up on the island of Isabella. The population of that island was somewhere around 1,400 people and 7 million roosters. I awoke the first morning to a cacophony of crowing, and my first thought was, "Aren't you supposed to wait until it gets light out?" Unfortunately, there's no snooze button on a rooster.

Imagine being Peter and waking up every morning to the sound of a rooster crowing. What a way to start the day! *Hey, Peter, here's a little reminder of your greatest failure! Good morning! Enjoy your day!*

Scripture says Satan prowls around "like a roaring lion" (1 Peter 5:8). I also think he crows like a rooster. He's the accuser of the brethren, and his tactics have not changed since the garden of Eden. The enemy of your soul wants to remind you of what you've done wrong over and over and over again, and then he wants to do it all over again because he wants you to live in the cage of guilt. He wants to hurl accusations at you and condition your spiritual reflexes with guilt.

Jesus came to recondition your spiritual reflexes with His grace so you are no longer living as a reactionary to your guilt. Instead, you are free to live as a revolutionary for His cause. He came so that you wouldn't be trapped in the cage of guilt and instead would be able to live the spiritual adventure He has called you to.

What does Satan's accusatory voice sound like in your life?

What are some areas of your life that need to be reconditioned by God's grace?

"The salvation and the power and the kingdom of our God and the authority of His Messiah have now come, because the accuser of our brothers has been thrown out: the one who accuses them before our God day and night" (Revelation 12:10).

EYE CONTACT

Let me highlight one little phrase in the scriptural text that is intensely intimate, personal, and relational, but is often missed in a casual reading of the story. Everything is in the Bible for a reason, and I love it when it says, "Then the Lord turned and looked straight at Peter." Have you ever noticed that statement? It almost seems like a footnote in the text, but I think it speaks volumes. The split second after Peter denied knowing Jesus for the third time, just as Jesus prophesied, Jesus looked straight at Peter and made eye contact.

What was in Jesus' eyes? I don't think it was a look of condemnation. I don't think Jesus was giving Peter the stink eye. I think Jesus knew Peter would beat himself up over this and made eye contact to reassure him that their relationship was still intact. Jesus wasn't about to give up on Peter, but I think He knew Peter might give up on Peter. I think Peter's denial doubled as his moment of greatest spiritual vulnerability, and that's precisely the moment Jesus made eye contact.

Listen to "Let It Go" by Tenth Avenue North on the *Chase the Goose* playlist. Your leader will send you the whole playlist via e-mail, or you can find it at *threadsmedia.com/chase-the-goose*. Use these songs as the background music for your study.

Eye contact is a powerful thing. When you look someone directly in the eye, a connection is made. Sometimes it's a good thing—like when you gaze into the eyes of the person you love, time freezes, and the rest of the world melts away. On the flip side, eye contact can also force you to come face to face with difficult truths. If you want someone to tell you the truth, the whole truth, and nothing but the truth, make them look you in the eye. It's more difficult to lie that way. And have you ever noticed how difficult it is to look someone in the eye after you've been gossiping about them? It's difficult to encounter them at the water cooler and make eye contact under those circumstances.

The fact that Jesus made eye contact with Peter in this situation says so much about His character. Jesus didn't even need to say a word. In fact, if Jesus had verbalized something to Peter, it would have exposed Peter as His friend and Peter would have been in trouble. In a powerfully selfless and loving way, Jesus sent a non-verbal message to Peter via eye contact. I think He was saying, "Peter, look at Me. I forgave you before you even denied Me. I just want you to know I haven't given up on you. We are still in this thing together."

I don't know what mistakes you've made. I don't know what sinful memories are etched into your cerebral cortex. I have no idea what failures form that cage of guilt in your life, but I do know this—God hasn't given up on you. He can't give up on you because it's just not in His nature to do so. If you can grasp that simple truth, you're going to be able to break out of whatever cage is holding you hostage. I think there are moments in our lives when we fail so badly we feel absolutely unworthy to receive the grace of God. Those are the moments that either make us or break us spiritually. Either we lock ourselves into the cage of guilt, or we experience new dimensions of God's grace that change our lives.

In what ways do you think you've given up on yourself? Do you feel like God has given up on you in those areas?

One of our core values at National Community Church is to love people when they least expect it and least deserve it. Jesus went around touching lepers, eating with tax collectors, hanging out with Samaritans, and befriending prostitutes. He reached out to the unreachable and touched the untouchable. He loved people when they least expected it and least deserved it, and we're called to follow in His footsteps. That's exactly what Jesus did with Peter; He loved the guy at the moment of his greatest failure.

When has someone shown you love when you least expected it and least deserved it?

Have you ever done that for someone else? When?

We don't give Jesus the credit He deserves as the Son of Man. He's fully God, but He's also fully man. Just think about what happened in this story. If your friend—your best friend—turned his back on and betrayed you at the moment you needed him most, could you forgive him? Beyond that, would you have the guts to hand him the keys to the kingdom? Would you leave him in charge of a movement destined to change the entire world? A movement you gave your life for?

At your small group meeting time this week, watch the teaching video "Breaking Out of Guilt." You'll see author Mark Batterson expand more on how Jesus reconditions our conditioned responses.

Listen to Part III of the audio conversation between the young adults of NCC: "Chasing the Goose in D.C." Your leader will e-mail it to you this week, or you can find it as a podcast at *threadsmedia.com/chase-the-goose.*

GRANDPA JOHNSON AND THE FOSSILS

My Grandpa Johnson left a tremendous legacy. One of my earliest memories is playing over at his house. It was a great house on the Mississippi River with lots of fantastic nooks and crannies for playing hide-and-go-seek. There was one area of the house that was off-limits, though, and that was my grandfather's fossil collection. It was essentially the tree of the knowledge of good and evil. I think I was about 5 years old when the temptation got the better of me and I couldn't resist any longer. I picked up one of those fossils and then dropped it. It shattered on the floor. It's weird, but I can still access the feelings I experienced so many years ago. It's one of the most emotionally imprinted experiences of my childhood. I knew what I had done was wrong, and I expected judgment. After all, my grandfather was a judge. But man, did he know how to show grace. He walked into the room and didn't say a word. He just picked me up and hugged me. That was it.

As a parent, I know there are times when you need to discipline. And you need the wisdom to know when to exercise discipline so it will bear the most fruit in your children's lives. But I think there are also moments when you have to love them when they least expect it and least deserve it. The grace you exercise in those moments will change their lives forever. The moment my grandfather encountered me after I dropped that fossil was my first picture of grace. I felt like my grandfather was telling me in an indirect, nonverbal way, "Mark, you are far more valuable to me than a fossil collection." It changed my life and I'm so grateful for that.

That's how Jesus loves us. When we least expected it, when we least deserved it, Christ died for us. That's what Romans 5:6-8 says:

"For while we were still helpless, at the appointed moment, Christ died for the ungodly. For rarely will someone die for a just person—though for a good person perhaps someone might even dare to die. But God proves His own love for us in that while we were still sinners Christ died for us!"

He didn't wait until we got our act together. When we were at our worst, God was at His best.

Do you feel like you can come to God when you are at your worst? Or do you feel like you have to get your act together before you approach God? Why?

Romans is generally regarded as the greatest theological document ever written. It contains the most complete explanation of God's saving work in Jesus Christ. In order to better understand Romans, consider picking up a commentary to help you. James Montgomery Boice's four-volume set might be a good place to start.

RECONDITIONED REFLEXES

Let's fast forward and finish out this story. In John 21, we pick up after Jesus was crucified and resurrected. He walked on the earth for 40 more days until the ascension when He returned to the right hand of the Father. During those 40 days, some amazing things happened. At the beginning of the chapter, Peter said to the other disciples, "I'm going out to fish" (v. 3). Now on one level, that could be a very harmless statement: "I like to fish; let's go fishing." But part of me wonders if it actually has a deeper meaning: "I think my career as a disciple is probably over and I'm going back to fishing." When we fail God, there is a natural inclination to say, "Let's just go back to what we're comfortable with. Let's go back to who we were."

There is nothing Satan would have loved more than for Peter to have spent the rest of his life on a fishing boat on the Sea of Galilee. He probably would have done everything in his power to make sure Peter caught plenty of fish so he would be content with a life limited to catching fish. But Jesus called Peter to be a fisher of men, right? And imagine the adventure Peter would have missed. The places he went, the people he met, the things he did, the miracles God did through him—what a life of spiritual adventure! There was a moment Peter could have gone back in the cage of guilt to live forever, but he didn't do that, and I think it was because of what Jesus did in this passage.

"When they had eaten breakfast, Jesus asked Simon Peter, 'Simon, son of John, do you love Me more than these?' 'Yes, Lord,' he said to Him, 'You know that I love you.' 'Feed My lambs,' He told him. A second time He asked him, 'Simon, son of John, do you love Me?' 'Yes, Lord,' he said to Him, 'You know that I love You.' 'Shepherd My sheep,' He told him. He asked him the third time, 'Simon, son of John, do you love Me?'" (John 21:15-17).

Peter was probably hurt. He was probably a little bit offended because Jesus asked him the same question three times. Maybe Peter's third response came from frustration: "Lord, You know everything! You know that I love You" (v. 17).

I don't think it's a coincidence Jesus asked Peter this question three times. Even though Peter was a little insulted by the repetition, I think there was intentionality behind it. Isn't it possible that Jesus knew something about conditioned reflexes before Ivan Pavlov came along? Peter failed three times, and Jesus reconditioned him three times. But that's not all. Think about when this story took place. In John 21:4, we read that it was "when daybreak came." Other translations note it to

Scripture specifically states that Peter caught 153 fish after Jesus instructed him to cast his net on the other side of the boat. Saint Jerome recorded that the Greeks had discovered 153 species of fish at that point in history, thereby indicating that there could be some significance to the number of fish caught. Peter was called to be a fisher of men, and in Acts 10, Jesus would instruct Peter that the gospel was to be spread to all men, not just the Jewish people.

John 21:15 is a widely debated passage among biblical scholars. The question seems to be over who "these" are. Some argue that "these" are the disciples. Others say "these" are all believers. Still others argue that "these" are the fish cooking on the fire.

Scripture tells us that Peter put his robe on before jumping into the water to run to Jesus. Jewish tradition considered greetings between people to be religious acts and required that the people be completely clothed. Peter was therefore preparing to properly greet Jesus.

be "early in the morning." Jesus reconditioned Peter while the roosters were crowing. From that moment, the rooster's crow was no longer a reminder of failure and guilt; it was a reminder of God's grace. The roosters stopped producing guilt and started producing gratitude.

Sin minus grace equals guilt. Without the grace of God, you are stuck in the cage of guilt. But sin plus grace equals gratitude. The grace of God is the difference between drowning in guilt and swimming in gratitude. And when your spiritual reflexes have been reconditioned by the grace of God, it frees you to come out of that cage, chase the Wild Goose, and live a life of faith.

As you consider your sin encountering God's grace, what are you most thankful for?

First John 1:9 says: "If we confess our sins, He is faithful and righteous to forgive our sins and to cleanse us from all unrighteousness." Maybe you've never done that. But I want to encourage you to look in the mirror for a moment and see if there is something you need to confess. There is One who can forgive you because He paid the price on the cross. The Wild Goose chase begins by simply accepting the offer Jesus extended when He said, "Come follow Me." It's as simple as saying back, "Lord, I don't have it all figured out, and I don't have it all put together, but thank You for Your grace. I receive it. I'm going to follow after You."

That is the moment when everything changes. In that moment, you don't just come out of the cage of guilt; you begin a new spiritual adventure.

For many of us, the cage of guilt is one we find ourselves in and out of all the time. I think Jesus would ask us the same question, "Do you love Me?"

I love Jesus. I'm so grateful for His grace.

If Jesus were to ask you, "Do you love Me?," how would you answer?

NOW WHAT?

PRAYER

Lord, thank You. Those two simple words seem to be the most appropriate prayer. Thank You for Your grace. God, I pray that You would help us come out of that cage of guilt, set us free by Your grace, I pray. In Jesus' name, amen.

SCRIPTURE MEMORY

"Then I heard a loud voice in heaven say: The salvation and the power and the kingdom of our God and the authority of His Messiah have now come, because the accuser of our brothers has been thrown out: the one who accuses them before our God day and night" (Revelation 12:10).

CHASING THE GOOSE

• Watch *The Lion King*.
• Begin a gratitude journal.
• Send some postcards to people in your life for whom you are grateful. Write one to God (you don't have to mail that one).

notes

THE CAGE OF
FAILURE

THE CAGE OF FAILURE IS WHERE MANY PEOPLE TEND TO GET STUCK SPIRITUALLY. When you experience some kind of failure—a failed relationship, a failed business, or some kind of moral failure—it's hard to avoid feeling like life is over. When you're in that cage, you tend to feel like you're the only one who has ever experienced what you're experiencing. I've got some good news for you.

Paul is an example of a man who refused to be caged by failure.

Let me set the scene of Acts 28. Paul was a prisoner on board a ship bound for Rome. For about two weeks, they experienced the perfect storm, and finally, their ship sank. It crashed on the rocks, but as Paul prophesied to the ship captain, no prisoners or sailors lost their lives (Acts 27:22). Everybody made it to shore. We pick up the story as Paul was recovering from the shipwreck—wet, hungry, and lost in the middle of nowhere . . .

Paul came to be a prisoner on the ship because of his role in supposedly inciting a riot some two years earlier. He was imprisoned in Caesarea for two years, then he invoked his right as a Roman citizen to be tried in Rome in the emperor's court. He was on his way to this trial when he was shipwrecked.

Malta is a small island in the Mediterranean between Sicily and Africa. It was colonized by the Phoenicians and later conquered by the Greeks, Carthaginians, and Romans. St. Paul's Bay has been identified as the location of Paul's shipwreck. There are no venomous snakes on Malta today.

Feel like you're having one of Paul's days? Maybe you can relate to the kid's book *Alexander and the Terrible, Horrible, No Good, Very Bad Day* by Judith Viorst.

TERRIBLE, HORRIBLE DAY

"Safely ashore, we then learned that the island was called Malta. The local people showed us extraordinary kindness, for they lit a fire and took us all in, since rain was falling and it was cold. As Paul gathered a bundle of brushwood and put it on the fire, a viper came out because of the heat and fastened itself to his hand. When the local people saw the creature hanging from his hand, they said to one another 'This man is probably a murderer, and though he has escaped the sea, Justice does not allow him to live!'" (Acts 28:1-4).

Now if I'm making up the rules, a shipwreck qualifies as a bad day. But the shipwreck was just the beginning. I've got to wonder if Paul is the only person in history who experienced a shipwreck and a poisonous snakebite in the same day. This is a terrible, horrible, no good, very bad day. Given Paul's circumstances, he could have justifiably developed a victim mentality: "Woe is me! What's going on here? God, if you're going to allow me to die by snakebite, why didn't you just allow me to drown in the sea?"

Instead, Paul chose to adopt a different attitude. He approached the situation as an opportunity for God to glorify Himself in a unique way, and that's exactly what happened. God has the ability to turn shipwrecks and snakebites into supernatural synchronicities that serve His purposes.

> If you were Paul, what would have been the worst part of the day—the shipwreck, the snakebite, or the bad reputation assumed by the islanders? Why?

> What's the worst day you've ever experienced? How was your attitude?

> What reaction do you typically have on terrible, horrible, no good, very bad days?

Let's continue the story in verse 5:

"However, he shook the creature off into the fire and suffered no harm. They expected that he would swell up or suddenly drop dead. But after they waited a long time and saw nothing unusual happen to him, they changed their minds and said he was a god. Now in the area around that place was an estate belonging to the leading man of the island, named Publius, who welcomed us and entertained us hospitably for three days. It happened that Publius' father was in bed suffering from fever and dysentery. Paul went to him, and praying and laying his hands on him, he healed him. After this, the rest of those on the island who had diseases also came and were cured. So they heaped many honors on us, and when we sailed, they gave us what we needed" (Acts 28:5-10).

Let me state the obvious—Paul and Publius should have never met. Malta wasn't even on Paul's radar, and that's not to mention that it would have been rather difficult for Paul, a prisoner of the Imperial Regiment, to secure a meeting with a government official. Even if he had requested a time on Publius' schedule, there was no way a meeting like that would have happened. It took a shipwreck to strategically position Paul at this exact latitude and longitude, and it took a snakebite to set up this divine appointment with Publius. The shipwreck and the snakebite weren't part of Paul's plan, but when you chase the Wild Goose, God just may use a shipwreck or a snakebite to set up an island-wide revival. Paul could have chosen to play the victim; instead, he chose to recognize God as the hero. Only God could orchestrate these kinds of circumstances.

Can you think of a time in your life when God used a bad circumstance to set up a divine appointment? Describe it.

Can you think of a "snakebite" or "shipwreck" in your life right now that God might be using to advance His purpose for your life?

The Book of Acts refers to Publius as the "chief official," or "leading man," of the island of Malta. His official position would have been governor. Tradition holds that Publius became the first bishop of Malta and later served as the bishop of Athens. Jerome recorded that he was martyred.

Is there an area of your life right now where you are playing the victim but need to recognize God as the hero? What is one practical thing you can do this week to move toward that mentality?

DIVINE DETOURS

Call me crazy, but some of the most enlightening and inspiring parts of the Bible aren't in the Bible. They are in the back of the Bible. If you have a study Bible, flip to the back, and in the appendix, you will see a section of maps. Most likely, there will be a map or two that show the paths of Paul's three missionary journeys. I'd like to call them "Paul's Three Wild Goose Chases." Look closely at the maps. What do you see? Squiggles. The one thing you won't see is a straight line. It seems like Paul zigzagged all over the ancient world.

If you read the entire account of his itinerary, also known as the Book of Acts, you'll discover that some of Paul's destinations were planned, but many of them weren't. For example, Paul ended up in Athens because a Jewish mob in Thessalonica ran him out of town. He traveled to Troas because the door was closed to Bithynia. And he landed in Malta because his ship sank in the Mediterranean. Athens, Troas, and Malta weren't places Paul planned on going; they were detours. But I might suggest that they were divine detours. They weren't part of Paul's plan, but God used what seemed like random and inconvenient circumstances to strategically position Paul right where He wanted him.

Look at a map of Paul's missionary journeys. What do you learn from them?

What does the map of your life journey look like? Draw it or describe it.

Can you see evidence of divine detours in your own life? Have you ever experienced a shipwreck or a snakebite? When it happens, it's

If you are really excited by maps, consider purchasing a biblical atlas. Check out the *Holman Bible Atlas* or the *Moody Atlas of Bible Lands*.

disorienting and painful. You ask, "Why am I going through this?" and it's only afterwards that you see how God used those circumstances to get you where He wanted you to go.

Honestly, if my plans had succeeded, I wouldn't be in Washington, D.C., serving as the pastor of National Community Church. I would still be in Chicago. My wife Lora and I actually planted a church there. I wanted to live there the rest of my life, but sometimes your plans have to fail in order for God's plan to succeed. When that church plant in Chicago never got off the ground, it was embarrassing and disillusioning. It was a failure. But I'm so grateful the ship sank in Chicago because God re-oriented us to D.C., and now I wouldn't want to be anyplace else doing anything else with anyone else. Plus, I don't have to endure those crazy Chicago winters!

Now, I'm not suggesting you sabotage yourself. You don't need to incite a mob against you or put a hole in the bottom of your boat. However, I do want you to understand that God often uses slow storms and divine detours to get you down the path of His calling and purpose for your life.

Several years ago, National Community Church was meeting in a D.C. public school. When the school was shut down for fire code violations, we were forced out. I thought the ship was going down, I kid you not. At that moment, the church plant called National Community Church was only a couple dozen people. The ship could have sunk and only 24 people would have ever known the difference. And truthfully, those people could have found a much better church to plug into. We could have ceased to exist, but God had other plans.

Forced to look into other options, we landed in the movie theater at Union Station. What seemed like a shipwreck turned out to be God's divine destiny for us. God opened up an amazing door of opportunity, and meeting in movie theaters became part of the DNA of National Community Church. But it all started with what seemed at the time like a shipwreck.

Here's the deal: When things happen in our lives that are jarring or disorienting, it rattles the cage. When we get a bad diagnosis, or a pink slip, or divorce papers, and the compass needle begins to spin, we start to wonder which way is up. It is in those situations that we need to realize the Bible says it rains on the just and the unjust (Matthew 5:45). Bad things do happen to good people. The good news is "all things work together for the good of those who love God: those who

Mark Batterson pastors National Community Church (*theaterchurch.com*), where the core values reflect a Goose-chasing mentality. Some of those values include:
• Expect the unexpected.
• Playing it safe is risky.
• Everything is an experiment.
• Do it right and do it big.

are called according to His purpose" (Romans 8:28). It's not that we are immune to difficulties and unexpected twists; it's that God can use them for His purposes. That's the promise we've got to hang on to.

> **How do you respond when people ask you, "Why do bad things happen to good people?"**

> **Who are some others in the Bible who experienced tremendous setbacks, failures, and disappointments? How did their stories end?**

Listen to "But For You Who Fear My Name" by The Welcome Wagon on the *Chase the Goose* playlist. Your leader will send you the whole playlist via e-mail, or you can find it at *threadsmedia.com/chase-the-goose*. Use these songs as the background music for your study.

I have a mental picture of Paul clinging to driftwood in the Mediterranean until he finally washed up on the shore. Sometimes the most spiritual thing you can do is simply hang in there. If you feel like you are drifting, lost at sea, or don't know where you are heading or where the detour is going to end, hang in there! I believe you're going to make it to shore. Sometimes the worst thing that happens to you can turn out to be the best thing that happens because God has a way of using troubled times to lay a foundation in your life and prepare you for what He wants.

> **"God wants you to get where He wants you to go more than you want to get where He wants you to go." What's your reaction to that statement?**

> **When difficult things happen in your life, what is the driftwood you hold on to?**

> **How might the troubles, disappointments, and failures in your life right now serve to get you to where God wants you to go?**

I would also suggest that sometimes we get so focused on getting where God wants us to go that we totally forget God is far more concerned with who we're becoming than where we're going. God is going to get us where He wants us to go—that's His business! But He's not going to get us there until we are ready to get there. And *who* we are *becoming* is far more important than *where* we are *going*.

Are you more concerned about getting to where God wants you to go or about becoming who God wants you to be? What's the connection between those two goals?

How are the troubles, disappointments, and failures in your life right now transforming you into the person God wants you to become?

At your small group meeting time this week, watch the teaching video "Breaking Out of Failure." You'll see author Mark Batterson expand more on the value of failure and how to get up after we fall.

AN ALL-AMERICAN FAILURE STORY

Some people face so much failure they inevitably feel like there is no hope of escaping the cage in which they're trapped. No one's life better demonstrates the ability to escape the cage of failure than Abraham Lincoln's:

- In 1809, he was born into poverty in a one-room log cabin that measured 16 feet by 18 feet.
- In 1816, his family was evicted from their home, and he had to work to support them.
- In 1818, his mother died.
- In 1831, he failed in business.
- In 1832, he ran for the state legislature and lost.
- In 1832, he lost his job and wanted to go to law school but couldn't get in.
- In 1833, he borrowed money to start a business and was bankrupt by the end of the year. He spent the next 17 years of his life paying off that debt.
- In 1835, he was engaged to be married but his sweetheart died and his heart was broken. It was devastating to him.
- In 1836, he had a total nervous breakdown and was in bed for the next six months.

To read more about the life of Abraham Lincoln, check out the biography *Lincoln: The Unknown* by Dale Carnegie.

"The probability that we may fail in the struggle ought not to deter us from the support of a cause we believe to be just; it shall not deter me."

–Abraham Lincoln

- In 1843, he ran for Congress and lost.
- In 1849, he sought the job of land officer in his home state and was rejected.
- In 1854, he ran for the Senate and lost.
- In 1856, he sought the vice presidential nomination at his party's national convention, but he received less than 100 votes. Ouch.
- In 1858, he ran for the U. S. Senate again and lost again.
- In 1860, Abraham Lincoln was elected president of the United States of America.[15]

Talk about the cage of failure! If anybody should have gotten stuck in that cage, it was Lincoln. He may be one of the most revered people in American history, but he's the last person I would ever want to be. He was a tortured soul who experienced an entire life of setbacks, sufferings, and failures. But those were the things that prepared him for the Civil War.

Friedrich Nietzsche said, "What does not destroy me makes me stronger."[16] I love that. Lincoln lost 40 pounds while he was in office. He hardly slept. When his son William died at the age of 12, Lincoln became incoherent and could hardly discharge his duties. Dale Carnegie, in his biography of Lincoln, said, "Year by year his laughter had grown less frequent; the furrows in his face had deepened; his shoulders had stooped; his cheeks were sunken; he suffered from chronic indigestion; his legs were always cold; he could hardly sleep, he wore habitually an expression of anguish."[17]

So here's my question—what kept him going? What allowed him to survive the personal and national crises of his life? I think a lot of it is that he never lost his sense of destiny. It's very hard to know what was going through the mind of someone who lived 150 years ago, but his speech before he went to take office in D.C. is revealing. I love these words: "I now leave, not knowing when, or whether ever, I may return, with a task before me greater than that which rested upon Washington. Without the assistance of that Divine Being who ever attended him [referring to the God whom Washington worshiped], I cannot succeed. With that assistance I cannot fail."[18]

Those may be some of the most profound words in our country's history. *Without His assistance, I cannot succeed. With His assistance, I cannot fail.* That's the sense of destiny that kept him going. And it's what will keep us going, too.

What keeps you going when life is rough? Find some examples of biblical characters who pressed on under extreme circumstances. What kept them going?

If you want to dig a little deeper into Paul's experience on the island, read the articles called "A Northeaster," "The Island of Malta," and "A Supreme Court Appeal." They'll give you some more context to the biblical account. Your group leader can e-mail them to you this week.

CONTROL FREAKS AND THE SOVEREIGN GOD

Any control freaks reading this? I'm not going to lie—I'm one. We like to use nice words to characterize ourselves, like "I'm a perfectionist" or "I'm a Type A personality." The truth is I want to control everything! I struggle with the things I can't control, and that's a lot of stuff. But here's the reality I must come to live in: I am not in control. That can either stress me out until the day Jesus returns, or I can gain the right perspective and let it determine the I feel.

You are not in control. On a scale of 1 to 10, write down where that statement leaves you on the stress spectrum. 1 = it stresses me out. 10 = it gives me peace.

If you are below five, how can you move toward resting in God's sovereignty?

If you think that one misstep, one mistake, or one failure can frustrate the providential plan of Almighty God, then your God is way too small. I'm amazed at my ability to put myself on par with God and think I can somehow frustrate His omnipotent plan if I don't do everything exactly right. God is bigger than that. The Wild Goose chase is an invitation to spiritual adventure; it's about saying yes to living the life you've been created to live. But it's more than that. It's a celebration of the sovereignty of God.

Sovereignty is a theological term that refers to God's complete and ultimate control over all the affairs of history and nature.

Proverbs 16:9 says: "A man's heart plans his way, but the LORD determines his steps." Take a deep breath. Now let it back out. That has a recalibrating effect physiologically, doesn't it? It helps us relax a little bit.

The sovereignty of God has the same effect on me. When I'm in the middle of a shipwreck or snakebite, I need to remind myself that God is ordering my footsteps. No matter how difficult the situation becomes, no matter how frustrated or disoriented I feel, I need to remind myself that God is sovereign. And that gives me a sense of destiny about my life.

One of the things I love about the Wild Goose chase is that life can turn on a dime. You never know when the Wild Goose is going to invade the reality of your life and turn it upside down. You never know when or how, but one trip, one meeting, one article, one class, one conversation, or one look across the room might change your life. You never know.

I've discovered our reasons for going somewhere or doing something are often very different from God's reasons for taking us there. When I originally moved to Washington, D.C., I came to lead a parachurch ministry. Now I see that God brought me to D.C. to pastor National Community Church. God always has ulterior motives; there are always reasons we are unaware of. Now that can either stress us out, or it can enable us to rest peacefully in the hands of a heavenly Father who always has our best interests at heart. Sure, it might involve some painful or difficult processes, but the truth is, that's how God gets us where He wants us to go.

God always has omniscient reasons we cannot begin to fathom. As the ship was going down, as the snake was sinking in its teeth, Paul must have thrown his hands up in the air and said, "God, where are You and what are You doing?" I think God probably would have said, "Hang in there a little bit longer, Paul, because I want you to meet this guy named Publius. In fact, his dad has dysentery and you need to go heal him and after that, everybody on the island is going to come to you. Then you'll have a captive audience and the gospel, the good news, is going to spread over an entire island . . . All because of that shipwreck and snake."

Describe a time when you did something only to discover later that God had ulterior motives.

WIND FACTOR
How did Paul end up on the island of Malta? It wasn't the navigational skills of the ship's captain. It wasn't the sailing skills of the crew. They landed on Malta because of something totally out of their control—the wind factor. Check out a few of these verses:

Listen to "The Time Has Come" by Hillsong United on the *Chase the Goose* playlist. Your leader will send you the whole playlist via e-mail, or you can find it at *threadsmedia.com/chase-the-goose*. Use these songs as the background music for your study.

"When we had put out to sea from there, we sailed along the northern coast of Cyprus because the winds were against us" (Acts 27:4).

"Sailing slowly for many days, we came with difficulty as far as Cnidus. But since the wind did not allow us to approach it, we sailed along the south side of Crete off Salmone" (Acts 27:7).

"When a gentle south wind sprang up, they thought they had achieved their purpose; they weighed anchor and sailed along the shore of Crete. But not long afterwards, a fierce wind called the 'northeaster' rushed down from the island. Since the ship was caught and was unable to head into the wind, we gave way to it and were driven along" (Acts 27:13-15).

"Because we were being severely battered by the storm, they began to jettison the cargo the next day" (Acts 27:18).

Headwinds, a light wind from the South, northeasters—you get the point. The winds seemed to be taking them off course, but it was the wind factor that got Paul right where God wanted him to be.

Things are going to happen that are beyond your control. You may lose a job, someone may break up with you, you may receive a bad diagnosis. In John 3:8, Jesus said:

"The wind blows where it pleases, and you hear its sound, but you don't know where it comes from or where it is going. So it is with everyone born of the Spirit."

In other words, if you are born of the Spirit by placing your faith in Jesus Christ, then the Spirit of God takes up residence in your life. You begin that Wild Goose chase, and you won't know where you are going or what is coming most of the time. And that's a good thing! It's right where God wants you to be. Jesus likened the workings of the Wild Goose to the wind. Sometimes it's a light wind from the South. It is nice when the when the wind is at your back. But sometimes it's gale force winds in your face. And I've discovered that resisting the Wild Goose is like spitting into the wind. You need to begin to cultivate a moment-by-moment sensitivity to the Spirit of God. In fact, you need to get to the point in your life where you trust His promptings more than you trust your own plans.

What kind of wind is blowing against you right now?

Another biblical character well familiar with "shipwrecks" and "snakebites" is Joseph. His father's favorite son, he was sold into slavery, then promoted to be in charge of his master's house, then thrown in jail, then forgotten, then given the second most prominent job in the known world. For the entire account, read Genesis 37; 39–44.

The Greek word for spirit is *pneuma*. Literally, it means "wind" or "breath."

You might ask, "But how do I know it's the voice of the Holy Spirit?" Like any relationship, you learn to recognize His voice over time. You learn not only to understand the words, but the tone as well. Think about the people you know best. With those people, many times words aren't even necessary. A look is enough. It's the same way with the Wild Goose. You get to the point where you can embrace the uncontrollable, unpredictable working of the Holy Spirit in your life. As I look back at the map of my own spiritual journey, I can honestly say I'm grateful for the shipwrecks and the snakebites. They were terrible when they happened, but they got me to where God wanted me to be.

Think about this: When Paul sat down with friends and family and regaled them with stories from his life, what stories do you think he told? How many times do you think he told them the shipwreck and snakebite story? Sometimes the worst experiences make the best stories. Why? Because God is sovereign. He is always at work and you've got to trust that in your life.

> Think of five stories from your life you want to pass on to your children's children. Do they involve anything like snakebites or shipwrecks? What titles would you give them?

"I am the good shepherd. I know My own sheep, and they know Me, as the Father knows Me, and I know the Father. I lay down My life for the sheep. But I have other sheep that are not of this fold; I must bring them also, and they will listen to My voice. Then there will be one flock, one shepherd" (John 10:14-16).

EXPECT THE UNEXPECTED

We have a core value at National Community Church: expect the unexpected. You just never know how God might work in a situation. You don't know when He might show up at the most unexpected time or place and totally change the reality of your life.

In 1921, the Philadelphia Church in Stockholm, Sweden sent a couple of missionaries by the names of David and Svea Flood to the Congo with their 2-year-old son. They joined another missionary couple named the Ericksons, and their assignment was to establish a missionary compound in the jungle. The location of their project was so remote that they had to use machetes to get back into the area where they were going. During their first year there, they didn't see a single convert, and the people in the area remained very hostile to the gospel. The native people looked to the medicine man and to witchcraft for spiritual guidance.

Every day, one little boy came to the back door of the Floods' house to sell chickens. And every day, Svea would tell him about the love of Jesus. Shortly after the boy started coming to their house, Mrs. Flood gave birth to their second child, a little girl named Aggie. Seventeen days after Aggie was born, Svea died. David was absolutely broken. He decided to take his son back to Sweden and gave Aggie to the Ericksons. He left and never returned to Africa.

The Ericksons raised Aggie for a couple of years, but when Aggie was about 3 years old, Mrs. Erickson died. Three days later, Mr. Erickson died. It was later discovered that the villagers had poisoned him to death. Two American missionaries named Arthur and Anna Burge took Aggie back home to America with them. Aggie grew up in South Dakota where the Burges pastored a church. Eventually, she attended North Central Bible College, where she met and married D. V. Hurst.

Fast-forward 30 years. D. V. and Aggie Hurst attended a church conference in London, England with about 10,000 delegates from around the world. One of the speakers that night was the superintendent of the Pentecostal Church in Zaire, now Democratic Republic of Congo, where Aggie's parents had been missionaries. He informed the audience that there were hundreds of churches and 110,000 baptized followers of Christ in Zaire.

Later that night, Aggie asked him if he knew of the village where she was born, and he said he grew up in that village. He told her that he used to go door to door selling chickens, and he always visited the Flood family. Every day, at the back door, Svea Flood would talk about Jesus. He eventually believed her stories and accepted Jesus Christ as his Lord and Savior. He continued to say that he had always wondered what happened to the Floods' daughter, Aggie.

When Aggie revealed her identity, he began to sob uncontrollably. After gaining composure, he told Aggie that he had recently placed flowers on her mother's grave on behalf of the hundreds of churches and thousands of believers in Zaire. Aggie's mom died so that thousands could discover and experience eternal and abundant life.[19]

While Aggie spent most of her life asking "why?" and wondering why her parents' story ended so tragically, God was working behind the scenes to bring unexpected results. Similar to the story of Paul, a seemingly pointless sacrifice was actually the catalyst for a miracle for thousands of people.

According to the missiological statistics manual *Operation World*, only 1.4 percent of Christians in the Congo were professing Christians in 1900. Today, that number has risen to more than 90 percent. Thousands of Christians and hundreds of missionaries were killed during the Simba Rebellion of 1964. Check out *imb.org* for more information about missionary work in the Democratic Republic of Congo.[20]

You never know how God might use something that seems like a complete failure. Here's what I know for sure—God has the ability to turn your failure into someone else's miracle. Isn't that what He did with Paul? A shipwreck and a snakebite turned into a miracle for everybody on that island.

"We know that all things work together for the good of those who love God: those who are called according to His purpose. For those He foreknew He also predestined to be conformed to the image of His Son, so that He would be the firstborn among many brothers" (Romans 8:28-29).

You're going to experience some shipwrecks and snakebites along the journey of life. But I want to remind you that God is going to get you where He wants you to be. More importantly, He's going to make sure you become who He wants you to be in the process. You are predestined to be conformed to the likeness of Christ. It's not just about getting to where God wants you to go; it's about becoming who God wants you to be. If you become more like Christ through the shipwrecks and snakebites, then even failures can be seen as success. Those things can't cage you; they actually become the platform for what God wants to do in your life.

I don't know what you've experienced, but if you're breathing, it means God isn't done with you yet. Remember, it's never too late to become who you might have been. Don't confuse a single mistake with a final mistake. God wants to take your failure and turn it into the foundation for how He uses you for the rest of your life. I don't care if it was something that was out of your control or a bad choice you made. God is bigger than all of that!

Don't buy into the lie of the enemy. He wants you to throw in the towel altogether. But if you confess your sin, God is going to heal you, He's going to forgive you, and He's going to continue to prepare good works for you. Maybe you are in a tough spot right now, but my prayer is that God, through His Holy Spirit, would give you an unshakable sense of destiny. He's not done with you yet. I believe I can say prophetically and biblically that your best days are in front of you.

What mistakes in your life are you tempted to view as final mistakes? What are some practical things you can do to come out of that cage?

Listen to Part IV of the audio conversation between the young adults of NCC: "Chasing the Goose in D.C." Your leader will e-mail it to you this week, or you can find it as a podcast at *threadsmedia. com/chase-the-goose.*

NOW WHAT?

PRAYER

Lord, help us. Help us. I know that there are a lot of circumstances, a lot of situations, a lot of failures that people deal with, and I know that it can be confusing and disorienting and frustrating and even embarrassing, but we receive Your grace and we thank You that You turn what could be final mistakes into single mistakes and You move us into the future.

God, I pray for those who are in tough spots. Maybe it feels like the ship is going down, maybe it feels like they got a snakebite, but God I pray that You would give them the strength to hang in there. Lord, I pray that You will give us the hope that You are going to get us where we need to go. I know there are some lessons we can learn and some character that can be developed in us that can't happen any other way, so I pray that You would work your purposes in us and through us and that our lives because of it would glorify You. We pray these things in Jesus' name, amen.

SCRIPTURE MEMORY

"We know that all things work together for the good of those who love God: those who are called according to His purpose" (Romans 8:28).

CHASING THE GOOSE

- Watch *The Shawshank Redemption*.
- Read *Failing Forward* by John Maxwell.
- Draw a map of your life and note where God's hand has been present. Reflect on what the zigzags may mean.

notes

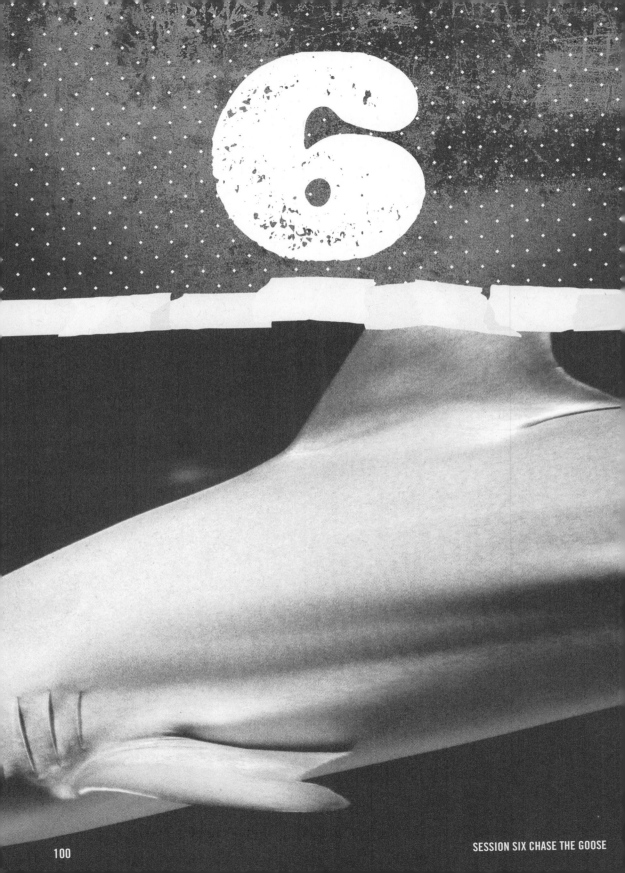

THE CAGE OF
FEAR

WE NEED TO QUIT LIVING AS IF THE PURPOSE OF LIFE IS TO ARRIVE SAFELY AT DEATH. Instead, we need to start playing offense with our lives. The world needs more people with more daring plans.

A few years ago, two psychologists from the University of Michigan, William Gehring and Adrian Willoughby, published a neurological study in *Science* magazine. They were interested in discovering the affect that wins and losses had on participants. In the experiment, volunteers wore an electrode cap while they engaged in a computer simulated betting game. Meanwhile, the electrode caps recorded changes in brain electrical activity in response to winning and losing. With each bet, the medial frontal cortex showed an increase in activity.

Read the article in the March 22, 2002, edition of *Science*: "The Medial Frontal Cortex and the Rapid Processing of Monetary Gains and Losses."

At your small group meeting time this week, watch the short film "Fear Protection." See if you can relate to anyone you see there.

MISSED OPPORTUNITIES

But the most intriguing discovery was that the medial frontal negativity registered a larger dip after a loss than a corresponding rise in medial frontal positivity after a win. (Are you still with me?) During a string of losses, medial frontal negativity dipped lower after each loss, and each loss was compounded by the previous loss. Moral of the story? Neurologically speaking, losses loom larger than gains. Or to put it another way, we fear loss more than we value gain.[21]

> **Do the findings of Gehring and Willoughby resonate with you? Why or why not?**

> **Why do you believe that losses have a greater impact than gains?**

That neurological study has significant spiritual ramifications. In fact, I wonder if that aversion to loss is why we fixate so much on sins of commission (don't do this and don't do that), while we often ignore sins of omission (what we would've, could've, or should've done). Maybe this is why we often approach the will of God from a defensive posture. We come to Him with a "better safe than sorry" mentality. Could that be the reason why we, as the church, are so often known more for what we're against rather than what we're for? We waste too much time playing defense instead of playing offense. May I suggest a paradigm shift? Let's quit playing not to lose, and let's start playing to win.

We need to fear missed opportunities more than we fear making mistakes. That's what this cage and this story are about.

> **Which is worse—sin of commission or sin of omission? Which is harder to attack? What is a sin of omission in your life right now?**

In what areas of your life are you playing not to lose instead of playing to win? What are some practical things you can do to start proactively and intentionally playing to win?

SCALING THE WALL

"Now a Philistine garrison took control of the pass at Michmash. That same day Saul's son Jonathan said to the attendant who carried his weapons, 'Come on, let's cross over to the Philistine garrison on the other side.' However, he did not tell his father" (1 Samuel 13:23–14:1).

I'm not sure if there's any significance to Jonathan's secrecy, but I find it fascinating because I live in a town where anybody will call a press conference anytime they do anything. I love the fact that Jonathan didn't make a big announcement about his intentions; he just went out and made stuff happen. It reminds me of Jesus' encouragement in the Sermon on the Mount: "But when you give to the poor, don't let your left hand know what your right hand is doing, so that your giving may be in secret" (Matthew 6:3-4).

Let's continue in verse 4:

"There were sharp columns of rock on both sides of the pass that Jonathan intended to cross to reach the Philistine garrison. One was named Bozez and the other Seneh; one stood to the north in front of Michmash and the other to the south in front of Geba. Jonathan said to the attendant who carried his weapons, 'Come on, let's cross over to the garrison of these uncircumcised men. Perhaps the LORD will help us. Nothing can keep the LORD from saving, whether by many or by few.' His armor-bearer responded, 'Do what is in your heart. You choose. I'm right here with you whatever you decide'" (1 Samuel 14:4-7).

It's tough to psychoanalyze someone who lived thousands of years ago, but I think it's safe to say Jonathan had a sanctified medial frontal cortex. He didn't let his fears dictate his decision. His desire to advance the kingdom was greater than his fear of failure, and his attraction to gain was greater than his aversion to loss. Jonathan wasn't playing defense; he was playing offense. He courageously climbed the cliffs at Michmash and picked a fight with the entire Philistine army. My New Living Translation captions this particular passage of Scripture as "Jonathan's Daring Plan." I love that.

Michmash is most likely the modern Arab village of Mukhmas in the West Bank, approximately seven miles northeast of Jerusalem. It is also referenced in Isaiah 10:28-29, in which it is prophesied that a terrible army would drop their baggage there.

This is not the only moment when Jonathan exhibited courage. In 1 Samuel 18, Jonathan befriended David, who would one day become king. He later protected David when his father, Saul, was trying to kill him.

Is your attraction to spiritual gain greater than your aversion to spiritual loss? On a scale of 1 to 10, how much are you playing offense versus playing defense (1 = defense, 10 = offense)? Where would you like to be on this scale by the end of this study?

The Philistines possessed iron weapons, which gave them a military edge over the surrounding cultures. First Samuel 13:19-20 tells us that the Philistines wouldn't allow the Israelites to make iron weapons. Israel eventually demanded God give them a king partially due to the Philistine militaristic strength and threat.

What is one practical thing you can do this week to play offense more?

One of the reasons I love "Jonathan's Daring Plan" is because it makes me feel better about my bad ideas. Let's be honest—this has to be the worst military strategy in history. Read the next few verses, and you'll discover that Jonathan's plan was basically this: Let's expose ourselves to the enemy in broad daylight and concede the high ground. Then, he devised a "sign" to inform their next move:

"If they say, 'Wait until we reach you,' then we will stay where we are and not go up to them. But if they say, 'Come on up,' then we'll go up, because the Lord has handed them over to us—that will be our sign" (1 Samuel 14:9-10).

Call me crazy, but if I'm making up the signs, I'm going to pick just the opposite: "If *they* come down to *us*, that'll be our sign." Or better yet: "If they fall off the cliff that will be the sign the Lord is giving them to us." But no—Jonathan's plan was far more dangerous, difficult, and daring than that.

Can you think of people from the biblical or broader historical record who have developed dangerous and daring plans and acted on them? How are they similar to or different from Jonathan?

Has there been a time in your life when God used you to do something dangerous and daring? How did it feel before? During? After?

Can I be honest? I'm just not as daring and courageous as Jonathan. And it really hit home earlier this year. My son Parker wanted to celebrate his birthday by playing airsoft. In essence, it's a game where you run around in an indoor arena and shoot each other with BB guns. Now, I'm not really into getting shot; it's just not my thing. But I love my son and he wanted to play, so we went. When we walked in, I knew immediately I was in trouble.

I was wearing jeans, but everybody else there was covered in full camouflage and some guys were sporting bullet-proof vests. I was seriously scared. So we played some games, like capture the flag with BB guns. When you get shot, you have to raise your arm to signal to others that you are "down" as you return to your base. The raised arm signifies that you have already been shot so your opponents don't continue to fire at you. Once you return to base, you have to count to 20 before you can jump back into the game.

I'm embarrassed to admit this, but I faked getting shot several times so I wouldn't get shot for real. I would hear gunfire and just immediately shoot my hand into the air. I would go back to base and count to 20 v-e-r-y slowly. It was surreal, and I started feeling really badly. I wondered if I would be that guy who faked being dead in an actual battle scenario. My lack of courage was astounding to me. Finally I tried to muster up a little bit of intestinal fortitude, so I grabbed my young son and one of his friends to plan a courageous act. I made one brave move and got shot in the chest. So I changed my *modus operandi*, and for the rest of the night, I would say to everyone, "Let me cover you," which was really just my way of saying, "You go ahead and get shot and I'll watch."

That experience helps me appreciate this passage, but Jonathan was in a real-life scenario. He was outnumbered and outgunned, and they were using real weapons. It took tremendous courage for him to climb that cliff. So here's the $64,000 question—what motivated Jonathan to climb this cliff? What gave him the courage to go on the offensive, and how did he know it was God's will? I think it's impossible to know exactly what thoughts were firing across his synapses that day, but

God has a track record of ridiculous and daring plans. Consider the story of Gideon, a general who was forced by God to decrease the size of his army time and time again (Judges 7). Or how about Joshua, who was supposed to do nothing more than lead an army walking around a walled city (Joshua 6). Then there is the most ridiculous plan of all—sending His own Son as a baby to be born in the midst of straw and animals.

verse 6 does reveal Jonathan's gestalt. He had a certain mind-set, a paradigm captured in that verse:

"Perhaps the LORD will help us."

I love that *modus operandi*.

GOOD OLD-FASHIONED GUTS

Let me state a personal conviction: I don't think what we're lacking most in the church is education. We need to keep learning and loving the Lord our God with all our minds. But most of us are educated way beyond the level of our obedience. I don't think our biggest need is resources. Let's keep giving, but we are the most resourced church in the most resourced country the world has ever known. You want to know what I think we lack the most? Guts. Good old-fashioned guts— to live by faith, climb the cliff, engage the enemy, and realize we're involved in something that is a matter of life and death. We lack the guts to realize we're called to live courageously and even dangerously for the cause of Christ.

Most of us have never been faced with nor will ever face a decision that would put our lives on the line. Nevertheless, passivity is not an option, and I think God is calling us to play offense. This story inspires me. It reminds me that the will of God is not an insurance plan; it's a daring plan. More often than not, the will of God requires a daring decision, a difficult decision, and sometimes, a dangerous decision that may seem unsafe and insane. People may think you are crazy.

I watch Jonathan climb this cliff in my imagination, and I can only assume he's a little nuts. But jump to the end of the story and read what happens in 1 Samuel 14:23: "So the LORD saved Israel that day."

> **What do you think is most lacking in the church today— education, resources, guts, or something else?**

> **Do education and resources give you more guts? Less? Why?**

Listen to "Daylight" by Jeremy Casella on the *Chase the Goose* playlist. Your leader will send you the whole playlist via e-mail, or you can find it at *threadsmedia.com/ chase-the-goose*. Use these songs as the background music for your study.

Is there something or someone in your life that you want God to save? If so, do you need to play any part in that?

One person made one move. One person did one thing that made a difference. May I suggest that the church needs more daring people with daring plans?

I like the way the 20th-century missionary C. T. Studd said it: "Some wish to live within the sound of Church or Chapel bell; I want to run a Rescue Shop within a yard of hell."[22]

The church needs more Studds.

What does your rescue shop outside of hell look like? What is it called? What does it do?

Charles Thomas Studd was a famous cricket player in England, where he played for Eton College, Trinity College, and Cambridge University. He worked as a missionary in China and was one of the "Cambridge Seven" who offered to assist Hudson Taylor in his efforts. He later served in India and Africa. He kept a postcard on his desk that said, "If Jesus Christ be God and died for me, then no sacrifice can be too great for me to make for Him." He also said, "The best cure for discouragement or qualms is another daring plunge of faith."[23]

When did we start believing God wants to send us to safe places to do easy things? Where did we get that idea? I think we make false assumptions about the will of God. One bad assumption we've made is that our spiritual lives should get easier the longer we follow Christ. Some dimensions of spiritual growth do get easier—practicing spiritual disciplines, tithing, and trusting the crazy promptings of the Holy Spirit. But in general, following Christ does not get easier. Spiritual growth prepares us for dangerous missions and to do daring things for the cause of Christ. Life shouldn't get less adventurous; it should become more adventurous.

"Perhaps the LORD will help us."

May I suggest that many Christians seem to operate with the exact opposite *modus operandi*? Perhaps the Lord *won't* act on our behalf. So we spend our entire lives at the foot of that cliff. We simply don't have the guts to climb it. After all, what if God doesn't act on our behalf? If we have that attitude, we're going to find ourselves standing at that cliff for a long time with nothing exciting happening. That's probably why a lot of us get bored with our faith.

In general, has your life become easier or harder since you started following Christ? What dimensions of your spiritual life have become easier? Harder?

In *Stand Against the Wind*, Erwin McManus seeks to help his readers react differently to the storms of life. Rather than folding and breaking, he believes we can stand firmly against the wind.

SITTING UNDER THE POMEGRANATE TREE

Let me flip the coin and look at the other side of the story. While Jonathan was out climbing cliffs, check out what his dad was doing in 1 Samuel 14:2:

"Saul was staying under the pomegranate tree in Migron on the outskirts of Gibeah. The troops with him numbered about 600."

What a study in contrasts! What Saul *didn't* do is just as significant as what Jonathan *did* do. While his son was climbing cliffs and audaciously confronting the enemy, Saul was sitting under a pomegranate tree on the outskirts of Gibeah. Can't you just see him popping pomegranate seeds into his mouth? Maybe fanning himself? Just chilling out on the outskirts of Gibeah at the natural spa.

Israelites considered pomegranates to be a sign of fertility and blessing of God in the promised land. Temple priests had pomegranate shapes on the hem of their robes (Exodus 28:33-34), and carvings of pomegranates were placed on the tops of the pillars in Solomon's temple (1 Kings 7:20).

The Philistines controlled the pass at Michmash. As the leader of the army of Israel, Saul should have been fighting back instead of kicking back. He was sitting on the sidelines instead of standing on the frontlines. And it wouldn't be the last time.

If you flip over a couple chapters, you find Saul once again letting someone else fight his battle for him. Saul was head and shoulders taller than anybody else in Israel, and he should have been the one to confront Goliath. Instead, he let a young shepherd boy do it. Saul should have been out on that battlefield fighting the kingdom's battles, but instead he sat on the sidelines as a spectator. Instead of playing to win, Saul played not to lose. And he was content to let others fight his battles for him.

In what ways do you rely on others to fight your battles for you?

Sometimes I wonder if we've turned church into a spectator sport. We are a lot like Saul, who let others fight battles instead of getting on the battlefield himself. We are a lot like the Israelites, who told Moses to climb the mountain and talk to God for them. It seems like we want someone to seek God for us, pray for us, study for us, and make decisions for us. If we aren't careful, we unintentionally foster a subtle form of spiritual codependency.

Don't misunderstand me—our weekly gatherings as followers of Christ play an important role in the spiritual rhythm of our lives. In fact, the Bible clearly says we should be together, "not straying away from our meetings, as some habitually do" (Hebrews 10:25). We need the synergy we experience when we come together and experience church. But do you really think God's ultimate dream for your life is to sit in a pew for 70 minutes every weekend? Listen to a sermon, sing a few songs, good to go? Is that as big as He can plan? Or is it possible we've turned church into an end when in fact it's supposed to be a means to an end? Church should be the environment where we rally the troops, where we are recharged spiritually. Sitting in church is not a barometer of spiritual maturity.

Spiritual spectatorship takes a variety of forms. Sometimes it takes on the form of doing the right things for the wrong reasons. For instance, I believe in giving to missions. It's the greatest investment we can make. But sometimes I think we are quick to write a check only to ease our conscience. We give so someone else will go. If God is calling you to go and all you do is give, then you are disobedient.

The bottom line is this—I think there's a little Saul in each of us. Part of us wants God to defeat the enemy while we are on the outskirts of Gibeah under pomegranate trees. I have a core value: Pray like it depends on God, work like it depends on you. Sometimes we've got to get up and do something. If we don't do anything, nothing is going to happen. Isn't that profound? If Jonathan hadn't climbed the cliff, engaged the enemy, and picked a fight, the status quo would've remained the status quo. We've got to take a little step of faith.

At the end of your life, God's not going to say, "Well *said*, good and faithful servant." He's not going to say, "Well *thought*, good and faithful servant." He's going to say, "Well *done*, good and faithful servant." We will be affirmed for putting our faith into action.

Here's the choice we have to make: Will we sit under a pomegranate tree on the outskirts of Gibeah, or will we climb a cliff?

Rightnow.org is a campaign designed to deploy anyone who is willing into areas of service domestically and internationally. Spend some time exploring some risky areas where you might be needed.

Those statements are found in the parable of the talents. You can read the entire story in Matthew 25:14-28.

What kind of fight do you need to pick with the enemy?

What changes do you need to make in your life to prepare you to climb cliffs?

Are you most comfortable with the idea that God would say "Well said," "Well thought," or "Well done"? How can you move more toward doing well?

ARMOR-BEARERS

Let me focus just a moment on the third character in this story, and the one who is most easily overlooked—Jonathan's armor-bearer. You might be thinking, *I'm no Jonathan. That's a great story, but it's just not me.* Every Jonathan needs an armor-bearer. Jonathan couldn't do this great deed alone. He needed his armor-bearer: "Come on, let's cross over to the garrison of the Philistines."

The armor-bearer said, "I'm right here with you whatever you decide."

And Jonathan climbed up with his armor-bearer right behind him, and together they wreaked a little bit of havoc for the kingdom.

We need more people like that—people who are with us heart and soul. We were not created to be on mission alone. Some of us are Jonathans. Some of us are armor-bearers. Sometimes we play different roles at different times. Most of us need to be serving as an armor-bearer to someone else.

Who is your armor-bearer? Do you think you need one? Why or why not?

Armor-bearers were chosen for their bravery. Their responsibilities were not limited to carrying armor, but also included standing by their commanding officer in times of difficulty or danger.

What leader are you serving as an armor-bearer for now?

What are some practical ways that you can help others climb cliffs and encounter the enemy?

The article "Philistia Versus Israel" will help you dig a little deeper into the conflict between the people of God and their enemies. Your group leader can e-mail it to you this week.

CLIMB YOUR CLIFF

I have no idea what cliff God might be calling you to climb. I don't presume to know the details, but I do believe it's daring and dangerous. It might not require that you go halfway around the world; it might be going halfway across the dorm or across the street or across the hall. Maybe you feel prompted to say a word of encouragement to someone in spite of prior fears you had.

Sometimes, it's the smallest prompting of the Holy Spirit that seems like the biggest cliff. But if you climb those cliffs, I guarantee the Wild Goose will meet you at the top and your life will take on an element of adventure.

While I can't tell you what your cliff is, I can give you some practical steps toward playing offense.

TITHE

I think tithing is a great way to play offense. I know what you're thinking: *If I give more, I'll have less.* No you won't. God can do more with 10 percent than you can do with 100 percent. From personal experience, I can tell you that your finances will turn into a spiritual adventure if you start tithing. Luke 6:38 says this:

The concept of the tithe is first seen in Genesis 14, when Abraham gave the Salem king Melchizedek 10 percent of everything he owned.

"Give, and it will be given to you; a good measure—pressed down, shaken together, and running over—will be poured into your lap. For with the measure you use, it will be measured back to you."

If you've ever practiced it, you know what I'm talking about. Tithing redeems the financial part of your life. It also relieves the stress because you realize through tithing that your financial problems are God's financial problems. He said, "Test me in this way" (Malachi 3:10).

Embark on a financial adventure and watch the ways God provides for you and glorifies Himself.

> Have you ever experienced a financial adventure? If so, what happened?

SET LIFE GOALS

You never hit a target that you don't set. I recently read an interesting book by Garry Kasparov titled *How Life Imitates Chess*. Kasparov won his first world-championship chess match in 1985, and he dominated the chess world for decades. In the book, he shared some of the lessons he learned. Here's one of them: "A Grandmaster makes the best moves because they are based on what he wants the board to look like ten or twenty moves in the future."[24]

That's a great picture of what goal-setting is all about. It's making moves now based on what you want your life to look like 10 or 20 years from now.

Let me come right out and say it—people spend more time planning their summer vacation than they do planning their lives. Instead of living by design we often live by default. I certainly don't want to over-spiritualize goal-setting, because we can set goals that are absolutely unspiritual and we'd be better off if we never accomplished them. But I also believe goals can be an expression of faith if we set them prayerfully.

I know people have varied personalities. Some people are natural goal-setters and others aren't. But I'm convinced one of the primary reasons most of us don't accomplish anything for the kingdom of God is because we don't have any God-ordained goals. And whether you are a goal-setter or not, Hebrews 11:1 defines faith this way:

"Faith is the reality of what is hoped for . . ."

> What are you hoping for?

Kasparov defeated the chess computer Deep Thought in a two-game match in 1989. In 1996, he defeated the IBM chess computer Deep Blue. In May 1997, Kasparov was defeated in a six-game match against an updated Deep Blue, and the match was captured in the documentary, *Game Over: Kasparov and the Machine*.

When you set goals in the context of prayer, it will change your life. Here are 10 steps to prayerfully setting life goals.

1. Start with prayer.
2. Check your motives.
3. Get ideas from others.
4. Think in categories.
5. Be specific.
6. Make a written list of your goals.
7. Include others.
8. Celebrate along the way.
9. Think big.
10. Keep dreaming.

Spend some time prayerfully thinking through and writing down 10 of your life goals.

1.
2.
3.
4.
5.
6.
7.
8.
9.
10.

There is a free download, "10 Steps to Setting Life Goals", on the leader kit that accompanies this study. Ask your small group leader to print it out for you or e-mail you a copy.

SERVE

In John 13, Jesus put a towel around His waist and began to wash the dirty, dusty feet of His disciples. In Matthew 20:26-28, Jesus said:

"Whoever wants to become great among you must be your servant, and whoever wants to be first among you must be your slave; just as the Son of Man did not come to be served, but to serve, and to give His life—a ransom for many."

"The only thing we have to fear is fear itself."
– Franklin Delano Roosevelt

I'm convinced God loves the smell of our sweat. I know that's a strange thought (and please, for the sake of your friends, family, and coworkers, keep using deodorant), but I think it's true. Remember, we should pray like it depends on God and work like it depends on us. God loves the sound of our voices when we are singing praises to Him. And I also think He loves the smell of our sweat when we are serving Him. Service is how we love God with all of our strength.

Sometimes serving others can be one of the most daring and difficult things we can do, especially when we are serving people who are not like us.

Maybe you need to go on a mission trip. Maybe God is putting a ministry in your heart, and you need to take a small step toward putting that into action. Maybe there is a need in your community that you can step in and fill. Maybe there's a place where you can serve in your church. Maybe that's the cliff you need to start climbing. Quit watching the game from the sidelines and jump onto the field.

FACE THE FEAR

Fear keeps us at the bottom of the cliff—the fear of disappointing others or letting people down. I face that fear every time I write a book. But I've got to face those fears. I need to pray, "God help me," and then do the best I can. There will always be things I simply cannot control, but I refuse to live my life fearing the things that are out of my hands. I'm going to face fears and I'm going to climb cliffs. And it doesn't seem to matter how many cliffs I've climbed; I still encounter fear every time I come to a new one.

Fear is one of the enemy's primary tactics. But 1 John 4:18 tells us that perfect love drives out all fear. So what do we need to do? We need to realize Jesus loves us beyond what we could possibly imagine and let that love grow until it releases us from the cage of fear.

"For God has not given us a spirit of fearfulness, but one of power, love, and sound judgment" (2 Timothy 1:7).

You need to face your fears and climb the cliff. That's the only way to experience the spiritual adventure God has called you to.

What fears do you need to confess?

Listen to the conclusion of the audio conversation between the young adults of NCC: "Chasing the Goose in D.C.—Part V." Your leader will e-mail it to you this week, or you can find it as a podcast at *threadsmedia.com/chase-the-goose*.

NOW WHAT?

PRAYER

Lord, I pray that You would give each one of us the courage to say yes to You, to say yes to the invitation that You have extended, and to say yes to the grace that You offer us. We want to say yes to those promptings of the Wild Goose and to Your plans and purposes. God, I pray against the fear, guilt, routine, responsibility, assumptions, and failures that keep us caged.

God, uncage us. Unleash us so that we can truly live this adventure You have called us to. Sanctify our medial frontal cortex so that we would be people who are not afraid to step out in faith. Forgive us for acting as if You may not act on our behalf, and help us live with the supernatural courage and confidence that believes "perhaps the Lord will act on our behalf."

We confess our fears to You and we pray that Your love would help us overcome them so we can become, so we can go, so we can do what You've called us to do, and at the end of the day, that we can hear You say, "Well done, good and faithful servant." We pray these things in Jesus' name and for His glory, amen.

SCRIPTURE MEMORY

"For God has not given us a spirit of fearfulness, but one of power, love, and sound judgment" (2 Timothy 1:7).

CHASING THE GOOSE

- Watch *Batman Begins*.
- Go rock climbing, skydiving, or some other form of adrenaline-producing activity.
- Spend some time journaling about your experience with *Chase the Goose*. Note specifically what you have heard God say to you and how you plan for your life to change as a result.

notes

END NOTES

SESSION 1

1. Michael J. Wilkins, *The NIV Application Commentary: Matthew* (Grand Rapids: Zondervan, 2004), 349.
2. Charles H. Spurgeon, *The Treasury of David*, Vol. 1 (Peabody, MA: Hendrickson Publisher, 1961), 171.
3. *http://www.whitedovebooks.co.uk/7-habits/stephen-covey.htm*
4. Korie Wilkins and Andrew Seaman, "Peace Corps Wish Fulfilled Years Later," *USA Today* [online], 12 August 2008 [cited 2 February 2009]. Available from the Internet: *www.usatoday.com.*

SESSION 2

5. *http://quotationsbook.com/quote/4892/*
6. Brian D. McLaren, *A New Kind of Christian* (San Francisco: Jossey-Bass, 2001), 122.
7. *http://www.brainyquote.com/quotes/authors/a/albert_einstein.html*
8. Elizabeth Barrett Browning, *Aurora Leigh*, edited by Kerry McSweeney (Oxford: Oxford Univ. Press, 2008), 246.

SESSION 3

9. A.W. Tozer, *The Knowledge of the Holy* (San Francisco: HarperCollins, 1961), vii, 2.
10. *http://www.awtozerclassics.com/page/page/4891821.htm;* James L. Snyder, *In Pursuit of God: The Life of A.W. Tozer* (Camp Hill, PA: Christian Publications, 1991), 228.
11. F.B. Meyer, *The Shepherd Psalm* (Whitefish, MT: Kessinger Publishing, 2005), 17.
12. *www.olympic.org*

SESSION 4

13. *http://nobelprize.org/nobel_prizes/medicine/laureates/1904/pavlov-bio.html*
14. Paul Tillich, *The Courage to Be* (New Haven: Yale Univ. Press, 2000), xxiv.

SESSION 5

15. The unsourced list, titled "Abraham Lincoln Didn't Quit," has appeared in countless publications, including a 1967 *Reader's Digest*. Read more at *http://www.snopes.com/glurge/lincoln.asp.*
16. *http://thinkexist.com/quotation/what_does_not_destroy_me-makes_me_stronger/11631.html*
17. Dale Carnegie, *Lincoln: The Unknown* (Garden City, New York: Dale Carnegie and Associates, Inc., 1932), 188.
18. Ibid., *Lincoln: The Unknown,* 121.
19. For the complete story, read *Aggie: The Inspiring Story of a Girl Without a Country* by Aggie Hurst (Springfield, MO: Gospel Publishing House, 1986).
20. *http://www.operationworld.org/country/conz/owtext.html*

SESSION 6

21. William J. Gehring and Adrian R. Willoughby, "The Medial Frontal Cortex and the Rapid Processing of Monetary Gains and Losses." In *Science,* vol. 295 (22 March 2002), 2279-82.
22. *http://www.wholesomewords.org/missions/biostudd.html*
23. *http://quotationsbook.com/quote/6637/* and *http://en.wikiquote.org/wiki/C._T._Studd*
24. Garry Kasparov, *How Life Imitates Chess: Making the Right Moves, from the Board to the Boardroom* (New York: Bloomsbury, 2007), 18.

DON'T MISS AN OPPORTUNITY TO LIVE A SPIRIT-LED LIFE

Most of us will have no idea where we are going most of the time. And although that is unsettling, circumstantial uncertainty also goes by another name: Adventure.

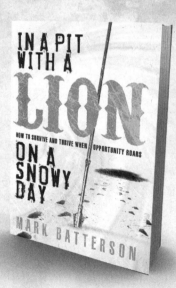

What if the life you really want and the future God wants for you, is hiding right now in your biggest problem, your worst failure... your greatest fear?

Find out what's holding you back and how to charge forward. For more information, visit www.ChasetheGoose.com and www.ChasetheLion.com.

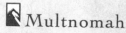 Multnomah

Keeping Your Trust...One Book at a Time
www.waterbrookmultnomah.com

take a sneak peak at another study from Threads..

RED EVOLUTION

EVOLUTION

ADAM THOMASON

RED REVOLUTION

[NOUN] A MOVEMENT THAT CHALLENGES CHRIST FOLLOWERS WITH THE QUESTION, "WHAT COLOR ARE YOU?"; A MOVEMENT THAT PROBES INTO WHETHER OUR CULTURAL BACKGROUNDS DEFINE AND LORD OVER OUR CHRISTIANITY; SOLELY BEING MARKED AND IDENTIFIED BY THE BLOOD OF CHRIST.

[VERB] CAUSING LIFE TO BE LIVED IN SUCH A RADICAL WAY THAT RACE, CULTURE, AND CLASS BECOME A SECONDARY ELEMENT TO BEING THE CHOSEN RACE OF CHRISTIAN.

FIRST CULTURE CHRISTIANITY
"BUT YOU ARE A CHOSEN RACE . . ."

For real, can you finish that verse? Most of us can't, let alone realize its implications. But the Bible calls us a chosen race. Imagine filling out a job application and finding the options of African American, Hispanic, European American, Other, and, that's right, the final race option of *Christian*. I believe the verse above is that literal. The problem is we have so allegorized this verse that we have looked past much of its meaning. In fact, I believe we should take this so literally that its interpretation causes the world to change—or better yet, it causes the world to *revolutionize*.

But let's say that verse should be seen as allegory. How have we, as a body of believers, been doing in America? Survey says . . . "not good." When I look at the history of the church in America, there is a glaring arrow pointing to the notion that, as my mom would say, "we got problems."

Go into the majority of churches across North America and you'll see the commonality expressed in various forms. There are the African American churches that have the small representation of "other" in their congregations. Or the European American churches that boast of the one or two black and Hispanic families coming to the church. Then there are the exclusively ethnic churches with one or two daring people who are trying to cross over but have no idea what the preacher is saying, because the "A" they got in Spanish was from high school. So they smile and nod "yes" to everything.

We want to sound diverse, but the reality is that disunity abounds. These token families seem to be little more than an effort to make ourselves feel like we are living out a gospel-centered message to all nations.

I'm being sarcastic, but these examples do lead somewhere—to Christ. I am baffled that we can look at these glaring issues of disunity and believe we are really living out Christ's Great Commission or Peter's declaration of the body as a chosen race. Instead, I think we're trying to make ourselves feel better.

BREAKING THE PARADIGM

Our culture has subconsciously conditioned us to accept three things when it comes to viewing life. First, the culture we are born into is the lens through which we must interpret life. Second, the culture of the world is the second one we must embrace in order to make sense of the one we are born into. And last but not least, the culture of our faith—Christianity—should be little more than an accent to the first two cultures. The majority of people live like this, operating according to those first two cultures and only seeing their faith culture as an afterthought. And we have fallen in line with the majority mind-set, even though the majority is walking in sin.

WE NEED TO UNDERSTAND THAT OUR FIRST CULTURE IS NOT ONE OF RACE, ECONOMICS, OR NATIONAL ORIGIN—IT'S ONE OF CHRIST. In fact, maybe we should refer to that culture not as *Christianity*, but at *CHRISTianity*. The term CHRISTianity is an intentionally new one, but one rooted in faith. It emphasizes CHRIST instead of the religious system we have created, exploring the timeless truth of Scripture highlighted through the Great Commission of Christ, Peter's statements about being a chosen race, and a smattering of other verses. Pulled together, we find a new—but also very old—ideology that can radically change the way we view and live life. First culture CHRISTianity breaks the mold of the American paradigm that has so adamantly and predominantly pressed its way into the body of Christ.

Just as our culture has ingrained the three above qualities in us, to live out first culture CHRISTianity we must do three different things. First, we must accept CHRISTianity as a literal race. Second, we must come to believe that race has its own and primary culture. Then third, we must view each other through the lens of Christ.

So whether you are African American, Hispanic, European American, Asian, or another of the world's many races, you are primarily defined by the chosen race of CHRISTianity. Everything else becomes secondary. Why? Because Christ—through His life, death, resurrection, and Word—says so. Last time I checked, our generational disobedience to this truth didn't leave the world marveling at the love we have for one another saying, "Man, they must be Christ's disciples."

TIME FOR A REVOLUTION

The revolution is happening. People are waking up to the reality that we have yet to live out the gospel truths concerning race. Race and culture have been our gods for too long, even within the body of Christ, and consequently, our lives have not changed in the ways they are supposed to. God has not called us to individuality while we wait for heaven, where we will be united as one. He has called us to see those who do the will of the Father as mother, brothers, and sisters (Matthew 12:49-50). Our cultural history has forged in us a dormant racism, an ethnocentric, separate but equal mentality, that is accepted and lived among Christ followers. This implicit separation is the furthest thing from biblical community and the exaltation of Jesus Christ.

RED REVOLUTION ULTIMATELY CALLS YOU TO QUESTION YOUR ALLEGIANCES. Are they to a flag, a country, a race, a culture, an ideology—or is your allegiance solely (like the title of the Derek Webb song) to "a king and a kingdom"? Are you ready to enlist in a revolution that is Spirit-led, biblically based, and challenges you to see the world through the blood-stained lens of Christ? The revolution is rising, and it starts with you.

WHAT IS THREADS?

WE ARE A COMMUNITY OF YOUNG ADULTS—
people who are piecing the Christian life together, one experience at a time. Threads is driven by four key markers that are essential to young adults everywhere, and though it's always dangerous to categorize people, we think these are helpful in reminding us why we do what we do.

First of all, we are committed to being responsible. That is, doing the right thing. Though we're trying to grow in our understanding of what that is, we're glad we already know what to do when it comes to recycling, loving our neighbor, tithing, or giving of our time.

Community is also important to us. We believe we all need people. People we call when the tire's flat and people we call when we get the promotion. And it's those people—the day-in-day-out people—that we want to walk through life with.

Then there's connection. A connection with our church, a connection with somebody who's willing to walk along side us and give us a little advice here and there. We'd like a connection that gives us the opportunity to pour our lives out for somebody else—and that whole walk along side us thing, we're willing to do that for someone else, too.

And finally there's depth. Kiddie pools are for kids. We're looking to dive in, head first, to all the hard-to-talk-about topics, the tough questions, and heavy Scriptures. We're thinking this is a good thing, because we're in process. We're becoming. And who we're becoming isn't shallow.

We're glad you're here. Be sure and check us out online at:

THREADSMEDIA.COM

STOP BY TO JOIN OUR ONLINE COMMUNITY
AND COME BY TO VISIT OFTEN!